EUROPAN15
AUSTRIA

PRODUCTIVE CITIES 2

RESOURCES
MOBILITY
EQUITY

PARK BOOKS

CONTENTS

- EDITORIAL 4
- LABORATORY OF OPPORTUNITIES 7
- GRAZ 12
- INNSBRUCK 34
- VILLACH 52

WEIZ 74
WIEN 92
JURY 110
TIMELINE 114
ACKNOWLEDGEMENTS 119
IMPRINT 120

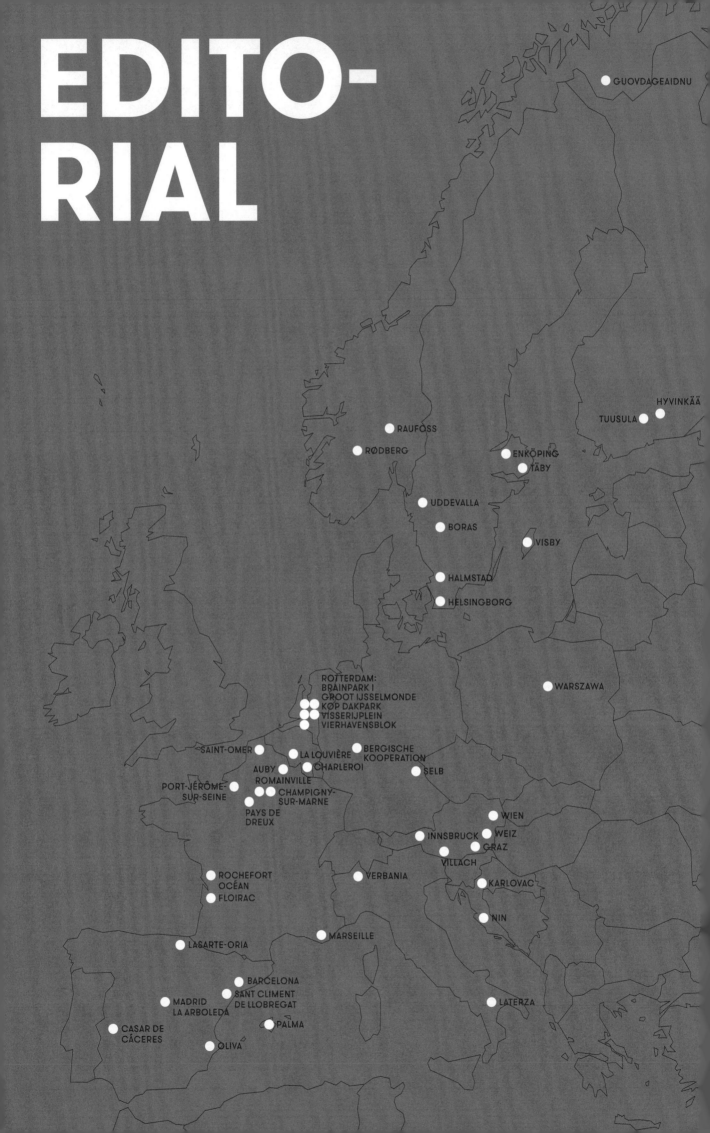

In this 15th edition of EUROPAN, participants from 39 countries contributed on the five Austrian sites. This implies an enormous range of perspectives being ingrained into the 123 proposals for Weiz, Graz, Innsbruck, Villach and Wien. A young generation of planners and a multifold group of experts are entering a discourse on the future of architecture and urban planning. With over 1000 teams participating in each Europe-wide round, a library of new ideas is unfolding. Almost irresistible for a young planner, EUROPAN provides a source of reference and inspiration and – most importantly – a chance to get involved and make an impact.

A significant component is set out: a competition to discover talented young planners in order to gain a fresh view, often from the outside, of challenges at hand. But the ideas of the young generation alone are not enough. It is equally important to understand that EUROPAN is one of the last bastions where discourse and competition still go hand in hand. In our fast-moving time, there seems to be hardly any room for this, although it is precisely this kind of profound treatment of complex socially relevant questions and topics which pays off in the long run.

The most important factor is the drive to lead the innovative ideas to implementation. It is clear that this challenge can only be mastered with a network of strong partners. EUROPAN has always been committed to nurturing a constant culture of exchange and promoting the passing on of knowledge between participants. In international forums, workshops and discussions all actors get involved from the very beginning, because the phase in which the competition is to be implemented is crucial and must be well prepared.

It is this moment between the celebration of the prize-winning projects and their further development, that this book was written. It captures an important snapshot in the process, explaining and analysing the nominated entries. Katharina Urbanek, in her comment on Weiz, recalls her own experience and feels the implementation phase is one of the most exciting and crucial ones. "In the months following the jury decision, the ideas and concepts of the winning projects are in negotiation, some will be pursued, even chased obsessively, others left behind." Blaž Romaniuk Babnik, also a former EUROPAN winner, reflects in his piece on Villach about the relevance of inherent possibilities of a site. He states that the potential of interpretation contributes to its richness, resulting in a substantial variety of approaches – apparent in the three nominated projects. The richness in Graz's site is seen by

Verena Konrad in the potential of an already rooted understanding on combining ecology, production and creativity. Integrating recreational activities – as asked in the brief – will set out for a "hedonistic-sustainability approach", as demonstrated in Copenhagen. On a more pragmatic note, Kristiaan Borret makes a stance to focus on what is relevant. "First things first" refers to setting the right priorities in order to anchor the complex site in Innsbruck. Departing from there, the development process will be able to thrive. Another complex site, and a site par excellence for this edition of Productive Cities, can be found in Vienna. Bart Lootsma discerns in the winning project a new era of a productive typology that is flexible and compatible with future demands. Moreover, it truly ingrains the topic into the city. "The brilliance of this project lies [...] in the forcing of an awareness of the presence of production in the city." EUROPAN15 is a second edition of Productive Cities encompassing the aspects of equality, resources and mobility. "[It] exposes the theme to ecological, infrastructural and socio-political premises, looking for an explorative 'value-mining', precisely related to the specific challenges of the respective competition sites", Bernd Vlay elaborates in his text as to why it was important to take the same topic to the next level.

In my first round as secretary general, responsible for tailoring the EUROPAN process for Austria, I gained a profound insight. What impressed me most was the wide range of participating actors and their openness to interact, exchange and learn from each other: young planners, city representatives, experts in a diverse field, local actors, universities, board members, councils, juries and decision makers. The most committed people come together to shape the discursive claim and put it into practice. This guarantees that innovative ideas are carried forward with the appropriate ambition and grounded in reality. A spirit truly needed for this great endeavour.

Travel with us in this book and see specific and deeply profound projects, enhanced by jury comments explaining their view and site representatives bringing in their local perspectives. Meet the new generation of architects, urban planners and landscape architects who are going to shape our environment of tomorrow. Be inspired!

Iris Kaltenegger is an architect and secretary general of EUROPAN Austria. She is the founder and director of Open House Vienna.

LABORATORY OF OPPORTUNITIES

Bernd Vlay

How to make an introductory note trespassing its representational role, mediating, just with a few lines, EUROPAN's claim of combining an ideas-competition with operational processes as an indispensable contribution to the future credibility of urbanism and architecture?

In 2016, with EUROPAN14, EUROPAN launched the theme of Productive Cities for the first time, provocatively asking for the comeback of a suppressed programme: for decades, the spaces of production have widely disappeared in the post-industrial image of "progressive" cities. Facing a considerable change in the structure and spectrum of production, EUROPAN asked for a possible re-appearance: could production open new perspectives and become an integral programme for resilient urban developments?

Two years later, when EUROPAN15 took the theme to a second turn, a change of paradigm had already started. In parallel to EUROPAN14, numerous EUROPAN cities were explicitly addressing the topic. Stuttgart, Brussels, Vienna, Barcelona and Madrid – to name but a few – launched important development initiatives dedicated to the topic, as they were seeing substantial values in the integration of the productive programme into city development plans.

Seen in this light, it is important to underline the special focus under which EUROPAN15 approaches the Productive Cities: the subtitle's terms Resources, Mobility and Equity expose the theme to ecological, infrastructural and socio-political premises, looking for an explorative "value-mining", precisely related to the specific challenges of the respective competition sites.

Thanks to the extraordinary work of our general secretary Iris Kaltenegger and her team, EUROPAN Austria could offer five EUROPAN15 sites. The following collage of quotes from all winning teams on all five sites lays claim to the creative sensitivity and deep engagement with which the teams have responded to the challenges of the competition brief:

> "... the yards cater as outdoor areas for urban manufacturing and facilitate social exchange... unlocking the potential of the city centre as catalyst for urban regeneration... a cluster of knowledge-producing-organisations such as the university and hospital working alongside with knowledge-hungry enterprises such as start-ups and scale-ups... considering the thematic concept of 'third space' as a threshold between the urban and suburban, celebrating the qualities of both... with a circular economy in mind, expanding upon local strengths, namely the pioneering attitude towards energy and climate, which has yielded world class industries and knowledge services... the creation of public space is a starting point for future development [...] to create a manifold part of town, whose neighbourhoods are connected... involving the public in the cycles of production, consumption and recycling, necessary to create a self-sufficient city... [in which] no longer makerspace is purely a space to use equipment but a space where people, materials, and ideas congregate to make new things... to define a process, not a mere project; a right mix of up-to-down and down-to-up

LABORATORY OF OPPORTUNITIES

solutions", in order to maximize its possibilities to be realised … a space, where ideas, materials, foods and energy are created, disassembled, repaired, recycled, processed, stored, sold, communicated and fed into cycles [...] consolidating the existing resources …" [1]

Quite deliberately I have put these quotes together without mentioning their authorship in order to illustrate that they form a common ground: all projects in this catalogue seem to represent a collective experiment, "curated" by the theme of EUROPAN15 and the implicitly shared concerns of the competitors, which might be named "site-specific value-mining". Based on a careful, multilayered and courageous investigation in the concurrence of local specificity and global discourse, the projects' value-mining aims at the excavation of the sites' potentials by exploring multifaceted and multiscalar relationships between physical, structural, social, cultural, ecological and political "things", scrutinising the spatialisation of material and immaterial processes. It seems that the theme of Productive Cities has been triggering synergetic representations beyond the bipolar figures of the architectural discipline. As Chris Younès and Céline Bodart put it in their illuminative text "New Possibles to Explore and Experiment":

Constantly moving back and forth between scales – from the ecosystem to the neighbourhood –, these representations provide us with an opportunity to rethink the process of transformation of inhabited milieus by examining the multiplicity of its agents and components, because they are natural and artificial, social and political, human and non-human, and … and …, and more specifically their modes of relationship, collaboration, articulation, interaction. [...] This new understanding calls for the establishment of new project communities and for the experimentation with new types of assemblages between knowledge and know-how, between make-with and make-together. [2]

Apart from the competitors' substantial contributions EUROPAN Austria was experiencing another make-with and make-together: we would like to thank all our partners for their extraordinary commitment and ambition during the competition phase of EUROPAN15. Their solidary efforts have contributed substantially to the making of unexpected horizons, tailored to the sites' opportunities.

With this catalogue the work on a promising future has successfully completed its kick-off. What has to follow now is the making of the implementation process. The winning teams are ready. More than ever, their projects need the local partners: the representatives of Graz, Innsbruck, Vienna, Villach and Weiz, who have been great "team players" in the competition phase. Now they are responsible for carrying the winning projects further on, taking them courageously to the next phase of implementation in order to keep the sites' promises alive.

EUROPAN very consciously stages the competition phase as a realm of ideas: a provocative frame, which animates all actors to imagine an engaged future, of which each site is a concrete testing ground. How can urban design, architecture and landscape architecture provide the things that are lacking? The lack of common grounds, of access, of a culture of publicness, of care, of inclusion, of biodiversity, of synergies – of valuable opportunities?

EUROPAN does not isolate this imaginative phase of assorted ideas, it is treated with careful consideration: implementation genetically inscribes

---

1 Selected quotes from the award-winning teams of the five Austrian sites of EUROPAN15, taken either from written texts or interviews.
Source: www.europan.at

2 Chris Younès and Céline Bodart: New Possibles to Explore and Experiment. A Palimpsest of Session Themes and Winning Projects, p. 33. In: Cities and Architecture under Debate. Europan. Edited by Chris Younès and Alain Maugard, Marseille 2019.

itself into the concept of the competition, transforming imagination into a programme of tangible action! Only if we take care of this inseparable link between idea and implementation, do we allow EUROPAN to become a laboratory of opportunities.

Seen in this light, I would like to make a final recommendation: ENJOY the projects, both as reader and actor!

Bernd Vlay is the president of EUROPAN Austria and a member of the scientific committee of EUROPAN Europe. He is an architect, urbanist and researcher, director of StudioVlayStreeruwitz, and teacher at the Academy of Fine Arts Vienna.

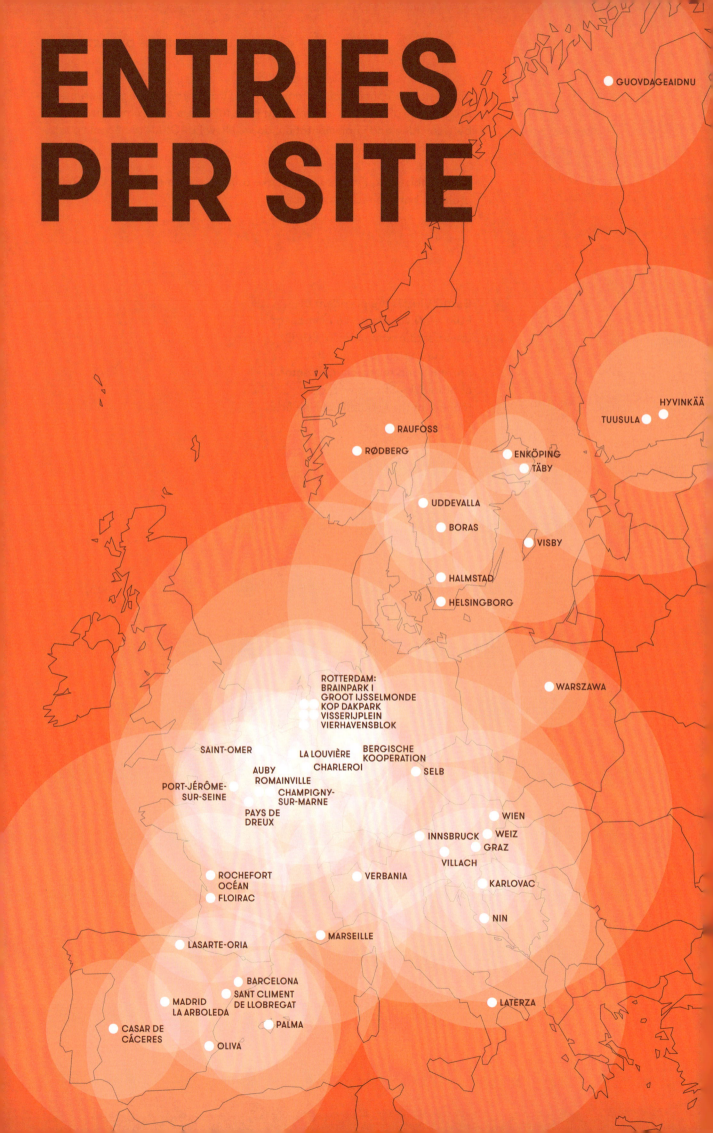

AUSTRIA	**GRAZ** 24	
	INNSBRUCK 33	
	VILLACH 17	
	WEIZ 12	
	WIEN 37	
BELGIUM	**CHARLEROI** 16	
	LA LOUVIÈRE 13	
CROATIA	**KARLOVAC** 10	
	NIN 22	
FINLAND	**GUOVDAGEAIDNU** 21	
	HYVINKÄÄ 16	
	TUUSULA 31	
FRANCE	**AUBY** 23	
	CHAMPIGNY-SUR-MARNE 20	
	FLOIRAC 17	
	MARSEILLE 18	
	PAYS DE DREUX 16	
	PORT-JÉRÔME-SUR-SEINE 13	
	ROCHEFORT OCÉAN 16	
	ROMAINVILLE 31	
	SAINT-OMER 12	
GERMANY	**BERGISCHE KOOPERATION** 7	
	SELB 16	
ITALY	**LATERZA** 28	
	VERBANIA 16	
THE NETHER-	**BRAINPARK I** 17	
LANDS	**GROOT IJSSELMONDE** 15	
	KOP DAKPARK 30	
	VIERHAVENSBLOK 20	
	VISSERIJPLEIN 43	
	RAUFOSS 15	
NORWAY	**RØDBERG** 15	
	WARSZAWA 8	
POLAND	**BARCELONA** 18	
SPAIN	**CASAR DE CÁCERES** 14	
	LASARTE-ORIA 43	
	MADRID – LA ARBOLEDA 10	
	OLIVA 26	
	PALMA 15	
	SANT CLIMENT DE LLOBREGAT 17	
	BORAS 12	
SWEDEN	**ENKÖPING** 8	
	HALMSTAD 17	
	HELSINGBORG 32	
	UDDEVALLA 11	
	TÄBY 14	
	VISBY 16	

47 SITES IN 12 COUNTRIES

GRAZ

A HYBRID PRODUCTION HUB AS CREATIVE MAGNET

GRAZ

SCALE
L – urban and architectural

LOCATION
Puchstraße, Graz, Styria, Austria

POPULATION
292,269 inhabitants

STRATEGIC SITE
48 ha

PROJECT SITE
2 ha

ACTORS
City of Graz, K2B Holding GmbH, Stadtlabor

— strategic site
═ project site

Two things are vital in order to understand the importance of the EUROPAN15 site.

First, its position within the wider city-structure: Graz consists of a beautiful old town surrounded by residential districts with industrial areas on the outskirts. One part of town, however, is spread across these different zones and defines a productive strip. With an average width of about 300 metres it is predominantly characterised by large-scale industrial structures. Its present identity has been historically shaped by a large number of important supply and disposal facilities for the entire city, such as the slaughterhouse or the waste disposal. Not only the central macro location and the water streams, but especially the size and continuity of the industrial band are important quality features. The local industrial enterprises can develop almost without any conflicts, despite the immediate proximity to the residential area and to the centre.

The second aspect is the development of a hydropower station within close proximity of the site, bringing the river Mur back on to city level. This big intervention is part of the "Smart City" concept that was anchored in 2013 as the principal strategy for future urban development. Graz's environmentally delicate topography – a basin surrounded by hills – calls for a low-emission city. New mobility concepts, resource- and energy-efficient projects paired with the latest technologies are key to achieving this goal. The prevailing mood for innovation is grounded in the raised awareness of requiring a sustainable lifestyle. The EUROPAN15 site plays a crucial role in this setting, being the most important fresh air corridor from the north. Two bodies of water, the Mur (main river) and the Mühlgang (small creek), run along it and

Site access road with the project site on the right – view from the east.

form a continuous urban biotope. The site's strip-like expansion though, doesn't support east-west connections, cutting off the housing area in the west from the main river in the east of the site. With the new hydropower station project the banks of the river Mur are to be remodelled and leisure activities are going to be introduced. The already popular north-south connection for bicycles and pedestrians will become even more important. All this will regenerate the area. The EUROPAN15 site will profit from it, thereby having the chance to create centrality in the industrial section, offer transversal links and improve the permeability of the site for the entire neighbourhood.

The EUROPAN15 site is embedded in an interesting field of diverse projects, allowing for an experimental approach. Old factories occupied by the creative scene can be found next to a waste site or a district heating plant – in between those, hidden places of beautiful and wild landscapes are thriving. The industrial zone found here is a paradigm for recycling and production in Graz, an area known as the centre of the 3Rs (Reduce, Reuse, Recycle) and the circular economy (cradle-to-cradle). The potentials of the surroundings are to be incorporated into the site, strengthening the character of the area as a lively, recreational and creative production hub by increasing the density of existing reduce, reuse and recycle uses. The demanding challenge of the task is working simultaneously on two scales. On the one hand, a strong urban design vision of the strategic site is expected, and on the other hand, an architectural proposal for a design and vertical densification of the project site into a mixed-use creative magnet is to be developed.

The project site property is built-up and has already been the subject of creative and sustainable re-use concepts in recent years. A former factory comprising of a two-storey office wing and a one-storey hall with a car parking area occupy most of the land. The Mühlgang with its enchanted wilderness borders the site and allows a glimpse of nature in the otherwise sealed surface. Part of the existing building structure has to be kept, as long-term tenants such as a coffee roastery and an artist's initiative adapted the spaces to their needs. Creating a hybrid of possible scenarios by incorporating the existing givens into a diverse programme of productive typologies is the task at hand. A cluster geared towards exchange and synergy facilitating work and recreation and welcoming a colourful mix of tenants.

As in the urban strategy, approaches to the productive economy and the sharing community as well as synergy effects within the environment are to be incorporated. Permeability, transversal connections and the integration of the neighbourhood are essential aspects. Concrete statements on functions and usage mix should be derived from the overall scheme and reflected in the architectural project.

GRAZ

BETWEEN MUR AND MÜHLGANG

GRAZ

Verena Konrad

The ambition of EUROPAN15 for Graz is hugely significant. The theme of Productive Cities required contributors to work on projects integrating manufacturing uses into urban development once more, an evolution that has already found its first expressions in the city. The site is perhaps not what we have in mind when we first think of Graz – an attractive, historic town centre, surrounded by residential districts with industrial areas on the periphery. However, the EUROPAN15 site is located inside the city boundaries between the rivers Mur and Mühlgang on a productive strip where you can find large-scale industrial structures with room still left over for expansion.

The EUROPAN projects find themselves in an exciting environment of change. Craftsmanship, especially when it involves reusing and recycling everyday objects, is coming back as a visible part of city culture. As well as production conditions changing, the whole work-life cycle is shifting. The lines between business, living and trade are beginning to blur.

Graz follows the "Smart City" strategy. Vital parts of that strategy are new mobility concepts as well as projects on energy-efficiency and the circular economy; aspects that are also important for the EUROPAN15 site. The project site property is well known in Graz as there have already been various ideas for the development of this area. A former factory occupies most of the land close to the river and parts of the building are already in use as a coffee roastery and artists' studios. EUROPAN asked its contributors not just to create a viable new scenario with a strong design vision for this site and its requirements, but also to find a way to concentrate all these existing rudiments. The creative scene is already there and has occupied formerly vacant spaces, there are small creative businesses and you can find the beauty of spontaneous vegetation in many corners. The approach of many of these existing businesses and initiatives is connected to a modern ecological lifestyle. The potentials of this area are high. What Copenhagen calls "hedonistic sustainability" is also something that can find realisation and expression in Graz.

The Milan-based team of winwinoffice was able to find a way to consequently elaborate on keeping land free with their winning project, *47Nord15Ost*. The core of this project is the plan to build up vertically and achieve density in this way, rather than sealing new surfaces. As a jury we could see the value of the project's approach, which was not simply a suggestion for another roof garden, but a merging of landscapes and a profound dealing with the matter of "earth". The proposal shows flexibility with many possibilities for diverse productive forms, a mix of functions, and various models of production that can be set by users and can be transformed when it becomes necessary. They worked on simple, open and adaptive rules that, in their words, "can bend to the needs of stakeholders" and act as resilient rules that "can actively respond to any economic, social, political, and climate variation" to re-generate a piece of the city in a suitably contemporary way.

As runner-up we voted for the project *Of Cycles And Streams*. The Mair-Paar Office For Architecture in Vienna started with the idea that, a "Productive City is a city of flows" referring to the "flows of resources, materials, goods, people, labour, knowledge, water and energy … that communicate and influence each other". In their proposal, the Mühlgang Hub acts as a "connecting point" for Graz. The team created a new centre here for the recycling and upcycling of a variety of resources. The idea of recycling and repairing also materialised in the transformation of an existing hall into a public courtyard. The proposal outlines numerous possibilities which can all find their place here: working, trading, creating, gathering, storing, or exhibiting. We could see a project here that is an intelligent adaptation of an existing building and creates a new typology of space in the productive landscape at the same time. It imagines a semi-covered plaza that allows the combination of production and public activities. It offers a new spatial potential to the city with its openness by creating an in-between space for a wide variety of uses and a strong and convincing typology.

The AMAA team from Venice worked on the proposal *Island (e)Scape*, which received a special mention. Their idea was to "re-activate the site offering quality public spaces for the residential neighbourhoods in the surroundings." They transformed the strategic site into multiple smaller islands. As a jury we appreciated their sensitive strategy to enhance and reinvent the entire area. *Island (e)Scape* relies on the unifying quality of landscape, finding objects to establish functions and link up twelve defined zones, shown as twelve islands in this proposal. The notion of connecting neighbourhoods found many expressions and different spatial advantages.

All three projects take great responsibility by recognising the value of the existing qualities of the site and finding expressions of hope and active transformation, which have me looking forward to the next trip to Graz in order to see this exciting transformation take place.

Verena Konrad was a member of the international jury for EUROPAN15. She is director of the Vorarlberger Architektur Institut and studied History of Art, History and Theology.

What are the main goals regarding the site?
The aim is to develop a centrally located, attractive, commercial location. The accessibility by means of soft mobility as well as the location between two watercourses provide excellent conditions for this. In any case, local use is to be intensified, with the intention of reducing sealed surfaces and increasing green spaces and mixed use. All in all the aim is to create an offer for companies in an urban location with excellent connections and an attractive environment, but also to improve the infrastructure for the adjacent residential quarter and for the leisure area along the river Mur.

How do you consider the issue of productivity?
Graz is a growing city with no outward growth in terms of area. An important factor here is keeping and valuing attractive commercial space because a growing population will also require growing jobs. The present area is part of a continuous commercial and industrial belt along the river Mur. An enormous quality of life can be found here both in terms of possible emissions, as no disturbances are to be expected, and in terms of accessibility due to its location on one of the city's most important cycle routes. The central goal of Graz's urban development is to implement the idea of the city of short distances, which requires productivity even in central areas and a good network of different uses.

Have you already defined a process following the EUROPAN competition?
The architectural implementation will be done by the owner*. No further sovereign planning is required at the present location. In continuation of the cooperation between the location partners, the city of Graz will provide support during the planning phase. The strategic objectives will be processed further on different levels. Individual measures, such as the improvement of passages and the networking of the same, will be incorporated into sovereign planning.
* First talks have been commenced.

Eva-Maria Benedikt is a site representative of EUROPAN15 for the city of Graz. She is head of the urban development and zoning unit at the urban planning department.

47NORD15OST

How could we reshape the future of a city to integrate public life within the productive areas?
Our vision proposes freeing up the soil through the densification of factories, allowing new public activities to happen in between, going from a traditional horizontal production to a new system of vertical factories.
A few punctual actions make the freed surface accessible, attractive and safe for the public in order to invite citizens to experience the 3Rs (Reduce, Reuse, Recycle) culture.
In order to face any economic, social, political and climate variations we established simple, open and adaptive building rules, discussed regularly in a participatory process involving all the stakeholders. Furthermore, the creation of synergies between the already established companies, and those to come, promotes the introduction of a circular economy model.

The future development of the area aims to create a new identity based on a shared, mature and democratic way of life.

*"When approaching the EUROPAN15 competition, we tried to find a balanced answer that could be positive not only for the productive district but also for the inhabitants of the neighbourhood.
Our aim was to define a process, not a mere project; the right mix of up-to-down and down-to-up solutions, in order to maximize its possibilities to be realised. We believe that the development of productive cities of the future should start from evolutive urban rules that can adapt within the economic, social, political, and climate variations. New industrial methods and the evolution of new professions require more and more flexible and adaptable workspaces. The hub is our vision to meet these new needs, an open grid, with maximum flexibility, where anything can happen."*

"A clear stance is expressed by '47Nord15Ost' resulting in building higher to keep land unbuilt." Jury

Right:
Visualisation of the finished project with the permeable open ground floor establishing a new connection between the canal and the "Hub" and allowing the building to be merged with a small forest.

PRIZE
Winner

PROJECT
47Nord15Ost

AUTHORS
Luigi Costamagna (IT)
Architect
Celia Cardona Cava (ES)
Architect

COLLABORATORS
Gabriele Cagini (IT)
Economist
Paula Camila Godoy
Gutierrez (CO)
Architect
Alessandro Talò (IT)
Architect
Lorenzo Giampietro (IT)
3D Artist

WINWINOFFICE
Corso Buenos Aires, 66
20124 Milano, Italy
www.winwinoffice.eu
Instagram: @winwinoffice

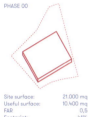    

Left:
Building development in phases, showing a successive change from the current volume to the new proposal, thereby integrating parts of the existing building.

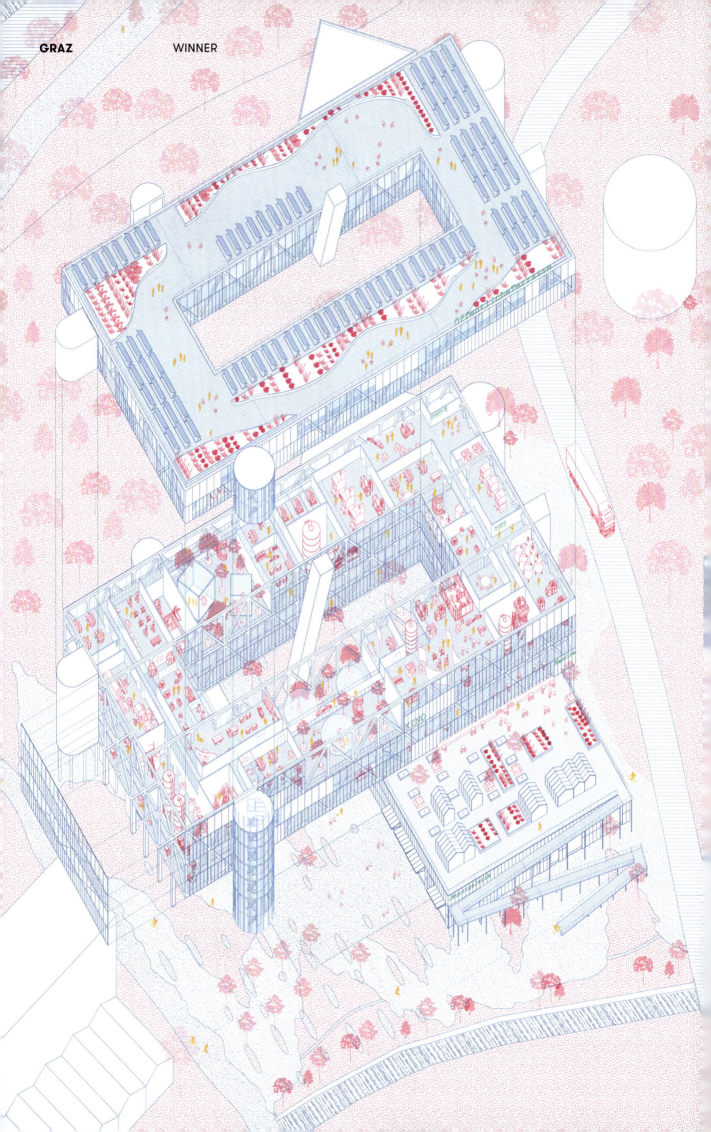

WINNER — GRAZ

Left:
Structurally autonomous from the existing building, the "Hub" is a radical machine, designed for its almost infinite reuse. Services, technical rooms and vertical distribution elements are placed outside the ring-volume ensuring a maximum of internal reconfiguration.

Above:
Visualisation of a possible productive scenario, showing a mixed, prefabricated structural technology of steel trusses and hollow-core slabs.

Below:
Changes cannot be immediate. The urban proposal suggests an interaction between constants and evolutionary rules. Sometimes a small gesture is enough, sometimes it is necessary to act decisively, sometimes decisions need to be rethought and taken in another direction.

JURY STATEMENT

For production to be kept inside the city, negotiation processes on a strategic level between the city and the enterprises are needed. With its hard and soft components, this project proposes urban guidelines for communal future developments. The idea of the circular economy has been dealt with by systematic thinking and consistently brought to different scales.

The jury unanimously values the ideological statement of the project and its consequent elaboration. Densifying is a sustainable option, because it allows land to be kept free. A clear stance is expressed by 47Nord15Ost resulting in building higher to keep land unbuilt. Its intrinsic approach to "raw earth" is rated highly because it is simply something more than a roof garden on top of a shed.

Besides that the flexibility of the proposal and the productivity brought into the third dimension are deemed the main assets of this project. It offers possibilities for diverse productive forms with a real mix of functions and various modes of production throughout the building. A generic spatial ring-volume is kept free of any logistic cores (they are located on the perimeter), thereby ensuring flexible horizontal and vertical uses. The generosity of the project is highly valued by the jury; however, it recognises new topics of logistic performance and usage that will arise with the opening up of the ground floor.

In general the project is considered an important and innovative contribution to the global discourse on Productive Cities and is therefore unanimously voted the winning entry.

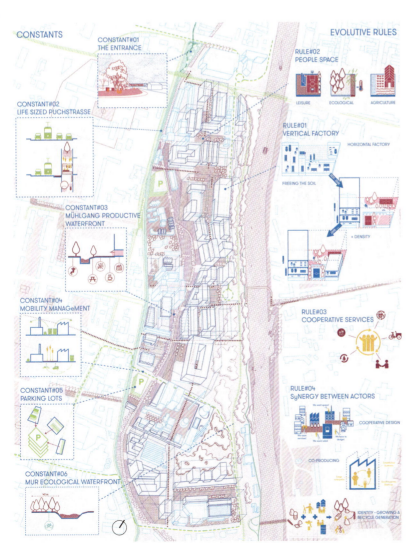

GRAZ RUNNER-UP

OF CYCLES AND STREAMS

"A Productive City is a city of flows." Flows of resources, materials, goods, people, labour, knowledge, water, energy, wind (...) communicate and influence each other. "Mühlgang Hub" acts as a connecting point for Graz's productive flows, enhancing the mill stream's potential as a productive vein. The new centre becomes a space, where ideas, materials, foods and energy are created, disassembled, repaired, recycled, processed, stored, sold, communicated and fed into new cycles. The existing hall is transformed into a public inner courtyard. It is a meeting point, market place, workshop, storage space, passageway, delivery zone and gallery. While the daily business is bustling, various production cycles are running in the flat base structure and micro-businesses are working in the towers above. "Mühlgang Hub" becomes the dynamic centre in a city of flows.

"We want to consolidate the existing resources and bring new qualities, new people and new awareness to the neighbourhood and the city.
The understanding of the idea of Reduce, Reuse, Recycle is essential to our project on all levels – from the concept for the strategic site to the existing warehouse, converting it to the atmospheric and programmatic essence of the new project."

Top:
Section West-East
1:2000

Right:
Visualisation showing the central hall, the existing artist's workshop and a spatial ring which promotes communication between the businesses by acting as a service zone; offering space either for a reception area or for small service providers or to store flexible furniture.

RUNNER-UP GRAZ

PRIZE
Runner-up

PROJECT
Of Cycles And Streams

AUTHORS
Eva Mair (AT)
Architect
Johannes Paar (AT)
Architect

COLLABORATORS
Sophia Garner (AT)
Student of Architecture
Giorgi Kharitonashvili (GE)
Student of Architecture
Elisabeth Weber (AT)
Architect

MAIR-PAAR OFFICE FOR ARCHITECTURE
Gaußplatz 4
1200 Wien, Austria
www.mair-paar.eu

GRAZ RUNNER-UP

JURY STATEMENT

The jury highly appreciates the internal square and the intelligent adaption of the existing building, thereby creating a new typology of space in the productive landscape. The semi-covered plaza allows productive uses to be combined with public activities and in that offers a spatial potential hardly found in the city: an open, inbetween space without a label, able to evolve and suitable for the area. The logistics of the place are well thought-out and are ingrained naturally in the ground floor area. Although the transversal public axis is doubted to be feasible, the access to the internal core seems viable from the side entrance. In this respect the proposal is deemed flexible, a reduction of the footprint could also be imagined.

Its expansion towards the mill stream is particularly viewed critically, as it leaves only a narrow strip of land and thereby cuts off the quality of the existing natural surroundings.

On a programmatic level, the project represents a traditional model, using horizontality to distribute productive spaces. It is questionable if the upper floors are fit to adapt to productive uses, as they appear more like office towers.

The urban strategy is only rudimentarily developed, although it does concentrate in a basic way on the two relevant topics, which are public space and transversal accessibility.

"The semi-covered plaza allows productive uses to be combined with public activities and in that offers a spatial potential hardly found in the city." Jury

Above:
The existing hall is transformed into a covered, public, inner courtyard, which is surrounded by a porous two-storey structure. Multiple uses are proposed.

Right:
Axonometric view of the urban situation showing transversal connections and a new waterpark in the building's vicinity.

RUNNER-UP **GRAZ**

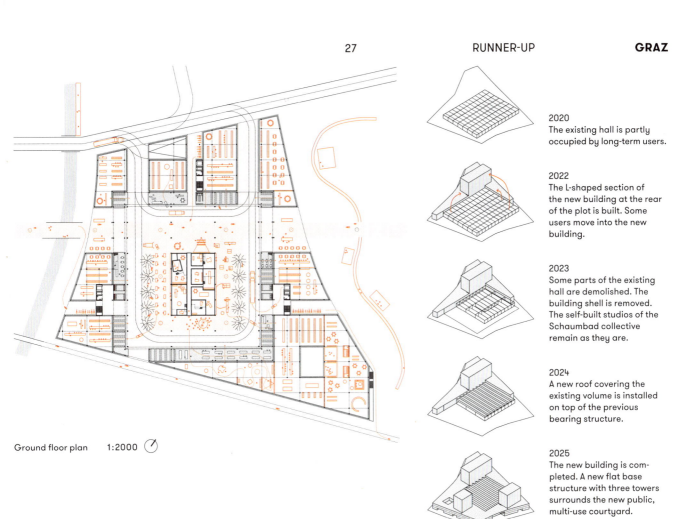

Ground floor plan 1:2000

2020
The existing hall is partly occupied by long-term users.

2022
The L-shaped section of the new building at the rear of the plot is built. Some users move into the new building.

2023
Some parts of the existing hall are demolished. The building shell is removed. The self-built studios of the Schaumbad collective remain as they are.

2024
A new roof covering the existing volume is installed on top of the previous bearing structure.

2025
The new building is completed. A new flat base structure with three towers surrounds the new public, multi-use courtyard.

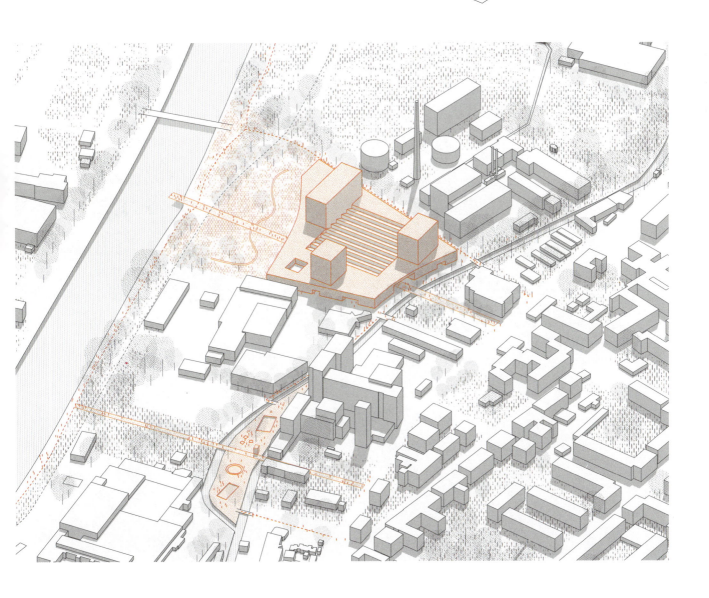

GRAZ SPECIAL MENTION 28

ISLAND (e)SCAPE

The idea is to re-activate the site offering quality public spaces for the residential neighbourhoods in the surroundings. This means transforming the entire island (the strategic site) into multiple smaller islands. The spaces in between will then increase the permeability and overcome both social and economic boundaries that still set physical barriers between groups of people today. We are talking about twelve islands – ten porous and two more private and less inaccessible.
The porous islands will be moderately transformed, aiming for increased usage and comfort. After the main Research Centre, other small buildings and constructions will keep pushing the site re-activation process: the main focus is on social and functional terms, leaving aside the aesthetic component.

"Our design process aims to weave a deep connection with the city, its history and its layers. It is not a unique and linear process but it is based on the continuous review of multiple options available, always keeping a critical attitude. Architecture not only reflects our time and culture, but also shapes it. The answer to any specific contemporary need or issue can always be traced back to old traditions, as in the urban strategy. Safe and easy solutions are not a reference, whereas the sincere use of materials reflects our attitude. Indeed, every part of the site possesses a unique set of challenges and opportunities to emphasize both the structure and the construction, regarded as the essence of architecture."

A new porosity is needed in order to add quality to the area. The project proposes looking at the strategic site as twelve islands which should increase permeability, based on the spaces between them. The industrial site is seen as a barrier between the residential district and the riverside which needs to be overcome.

PRIZE
Special Mention

PROJECT
Island (e)Scape

AUTHORS
Alessandra Rampazzo (IT)
Architect
Susanna Aina Lindvall (SE)
Architect
Luca Negrini (IT)
Architect
Marcello Galiotto (IT)
Architect

COLLABORATORS
Yasmine Houari (BE)
Architect
Francesco Cauda (IT)
Student of Architecture
Carlotta Floreano (IT)
Student of Architecture
Francesco Baggio (IT)
Student of Architecture

AMAA
San Marco 2504
30124 Venezia, Italy
www.amaa.studio

"The project's underlying notion of connectedness permeates the entire neighbourhood and is exercised on a variety of scales and using different tools." Jury

2019 TODAY

2025
+20% DENSITY

2040
+30% DENSITY

2050
+50% DENSITY

2060
+70% DENSITY

2100 FUTURAMA
+100% DENSITY

GRAZ SPECIAL MENTION 30

TOOLS

01 INNOVATION CENTRE

Two blocks elevated on a permeable basement host the programme related to the research centre.

02 SPORT CENTRE

A built island connected to the other islands through ramps and bridges. It hosts the facilities of a sport centre and has the technology to produce green energy.

03 MOBILITY HUB

This building is both a mobility hub and a new mobility gate for the urban surroundings thanks to its site specific location.

04 PERMANENT CIRCUS

A building made for entertainment: it is flexible and can be adapted to selected requirements for a wide variety of events.

05 CAGE

A building that looks like a cage: perfect as a boxing ring, a trampoline, a colourful ball pool for kids.

06 SPORT FIELD

An area dedicated to a playground. It can be used in combination with another tool or put inside a green area.

07 GATE/WALL

In private and protected areas, power plant and the slaughterhouse, a wall takes place along the edges and interrupted with gates strategically located.

08 GABLE ROOF

The roof defines a space that can be used for public activities like the street market or be a plus for existing small retails.

09 FLAT ROOF

The roof defines a space that can be used for public activities like the street market or be a plus for existing small retails.

10 URBAN CENTRE/CAFÉ

A place dedicated to people and their needs to gather as a community. The covered and closed space can be adapted to multiple uses.

11 BUS STOP

Recognizable small and simple element with the basic function of protecting people waiting for the bus.

12 BENCH

The smallest element of this toolkit is the main one to increase the interaction amongst people.

JURY STATEMENT

The project's urban take and its sensitive and strategic approach towards the entire area is highly convincing. *Island (e)Scape* works with the unifying aspect of the landscape, in which single, distinct objects define functional, aesthetic and atmospheric bridges between 12 zones – 12 islands. The project's underlying notion of connectedness permeates the entire neighbourhood and is exercised on a variety of scales and tools, each of them treated equally. Thus, different spatial qualities arise upon the interventions and open up unexpected possibilities.

The programming remains flexible and open, operating with a system of jigsaw pieces. The transformation from the urban analysis into the proposed architectural project is insufficient. The programmatic distribution, its relation to the surroundings and its assigned volumes remain unclear or unsuitable. Emphasis is put on the vertical mix with big spaces for production on the ground floor. Still, the spirit of the urban is not tangible in the architectural proposal and this doesn't offer a convincing solution for the site.

SPECIAL MENTION — GRAZ

Far left:
The regeneration process is envisaged to start in 2025 and will gradually involve the entire strategic site and urban surroundings. Over the years a toolkit of diverse elements will activate each island – one after the other – in a sequence of upgrades which will help integrate the industrial site into the urban evolution.

Left:
The plan shows the interventions anchored on site.

Top:
A new research centre becomes the starting point for the development of the circular economy which will help to regenerate the entire strategic site. The new building merges with the existing one, it will be rich in complexity and should be a new landmark. The creek is developed into a recreation area for residents.

Above:
A variety of future scenarios is possible. Open air levels with façades permeable to the air can be adapted for farming, as shown here.

PARTICIPANTS AND WINNERS
IN TOTAL

REGISTRATIONS 1241

ENTRIES 901

SHORTLIST 230

PRIZES 136

RUNNERS-UP 47
WINNERS 44

INN'SITE

INNSBRUCK

SCALE
L – urban and architectural

LOCATION
Innrain, Innsbruck, Tyrol, Austria

POPULATION
City: 133,540
Conurbation: 156,690

STRATEGIC SITE
18 ha

PROJECT SITE
3.2 ha

ACTORS
City of Innsbruck,
IIG Innsbrucker Immobiliengesellschaft

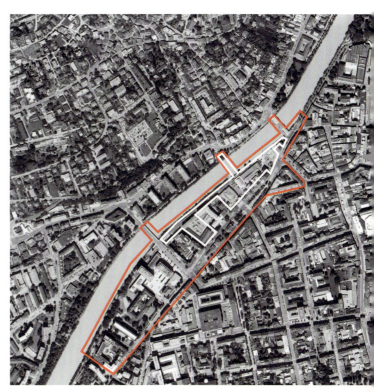

— strategic site
▭ project site

Innsbruck's newly elected government has a very ambitious plan for the city. Goals are already set for soft mobility, sustainability, densification and reuse, green and open spaces, job preservation and creation, and participation. Everything is geared towards a resilient city within short distances. The EUROPAN15 site doesn't just sit inside this progressive framework of ideas, it is perfectly located on a central spot in town where all of the previously mentioned ideas come together at once. Also, the river "Inn", which gives the city its name, plays a key role when discussing the site and contributes additionally to the highly complex setting. Many aspects are to be negotiated: identity, connections, sequences, volumes and voids, mobility, uses and use conditions, to name a few. A field of diverse, yet promising, fragments is laid out here. They need to be considered carefully and bundled, in order to bring the power of place back to this location.

For one, the EUROPAN15 site faces the most picturesque scenery of Innsbruck – colourful housing with huge mountains in the background: its market square, a vast empty place, offers the best view onto this postcard-like vista and is therefore a hotspot for tourists. The site's enormous potential though is barely used despite its prime location. The site comprises of important components, such as the extensive market square and a charming market hall which could be improved upon, a parking garage (to be removed) and a huge office block (soon to be vacated). Inevitably, due to being surrounded by mountains, the compact city has limited spatial resources. Densification, re-use and restructuring built-up areas are therefore main objectives for the urban development. An open space of similar dimensions, relating to the scenery and functioning as a window to peek out into the landscape like the market square does, cannot be found elsewhere in the city. The handling of the square will be critical. Its emptiness evokes opportunities and triggers investigations into sequences of open and built spaces, which become especially important to create a pattern of permeability connecting the surrounding city-fabric with the site.

INNSBRUCK

The project site is a long area stretched out between the river Inn and a busy street splitting it off from the old town. In recent years, the amount of traffic has risen constantly, accumulating in a neuralgic point at the junction next to the market square, at the eastern part of the site. It is a pivotal point where several mobility strands cross and by-pass, disturbing and interrupting uses. Still, the site is well frequented and well-known by every inhabitant of Innsbruck. It is so central it seems everything happens here: there are tourists, bikes, cars, cafés, shops, a market, restaurants and people strolling around. Nonetheless it lacks identity.

Innsbruck's ambition "to bring the river Inn back to the city" is talking about connections on yet another level. With this powerful river bordering the site, the topic of the waterscape is essential. Although the river runs directly through the city, only limited access points are available. Due to natural circumstances, the water level can rise enormously, especially in spring and rainy seasons. Strict safety regulations are therefore in place. Most of the year the presence of the river is not tangible in an actual and direct sense: there is no riverbank to stroll along and the water level is some ten metres safely below the city. Nevertheless, it is powerful through its sheer width and expansion. In the past the river was used for shipping, nowadays there are a couple of hydroelectric power stations along its course. This body of water still represents one of the most important infrastructures of the city and is part of the urban ecology. The imminent strength of an alpine stream might support and enrich the discussion of productive uses.

Productive uses – the subtheme of this site – addresses uses that go beyond solely functional activities and act as more of an urban generator triggering new life and new dynamics. A profound and integral approach which knits existing and new uses together into the site will be crucial. What kind of uses can be imagined or are attainable in the very context of the EUROPAN15 site? A wide range already exists in the vicinity, such as the university, the market hall, the square, the hospital, the old town, the opposite side of the river and other institutions. All of these can develop great potential once possible synergies are expanded upon and new proximities of programmes are accommodated; mixing different actors and young entrepreneurs together in new collaborations and accentuating existing resources in culture, education and business by joining them up with other functions which may arise, not from planning but rather by enabling. Above all the definition of spaces must be informed by use and result from linking them with programme.

Market Square with its
main view of the
opposite river bank and
the mountains

INNSBRUCK

THE MARKTPLATZ

INNSBRUCK

Kristiaan Borret

The Marktplatz. What wonderful fantasies that place name puts to work in our minds! And what's more, in Innsbruck. It's one of those central European cities where the spaces are well proportioned and where Camillo Sitte can't live up to its picturesque happiness, with urban plinths which Jane Jacobs would appreciate, and now and then a contemporary intervention that seeks out some tasteful dissonance, as Zaha showed us.

Well, it's nothing like that when you arrive at the real Marktplatz in Innsbruck. It's an ugly oversized space, with a poorly camouflaged pumping station and a market hall building that closes off to the outside. Luckily there is the beautiful view over the Inn to the other side with the mountains in the background.

So 'first things first' for the competition participants: make a good square!

That probably starts with a better outline of the square. Today the space is undefined and so both runners-up make a first move by making the square smaller. In the proposal *Das Grüne Herz* by means of a kind of pergola that also shields the place from the traffic to fully direct it towards the waterfront. Or by dividing the space into a big square and a little square. Indeed, *Happy Valley* makes the first one lightly tilting and the second gets covered with an industrial looking canopy. Even though open space is a scarce commodity in a dense city, both designs show that a good public space benefits from being reduced in order to be well dimensioned, and all the more intensely to play its role. I would prefer the right focus with a smaller square than preserving everything that is open today, but then condemning it to be shapeless forever.

> "So 'first things first' for the competition participants: make a good square!"

In *Happy Valley* a type of building is being explored that does not yet exist in Innsbruck, neither in terms of form nor programme. It is a hybrid between building and public space, between infrastructure and programme, between present and past. The place needs an innovative programming and the project does that by looking for public-oriented activities that might activate the new square. A new centre for Food Urbanism gathers all kinds of functions that promote a healthy lifestyle. It sounds pertinent, but hopefully it won't end up as a kind of high-end hipster consumerism. It touches on the idea that a city should be productive, but it doesn't really go in the direction of making room in the city for a productive economy that employs blue collars. Even though the Productive City is an objective which many people in Europe – including me in Brussels – have put on the agenda, it is right to give priority in this place to getting the handling of public space in order and integrating it with uses that generate identity and liveliness.

Das Grüne Herz goes in a different direction and emphasises the continuity of public space in the urban fabric as a whole. For example, they articulate a clear promenade along the water's edge, which strings together a series of new urban programmes like a cord. In this way, the promenade along the university buildings further upstream is completed to form a large figure in which the Marktplatz is a very special one of many special moments. Also, in the transversal direction, the permeability of the existing urban structure is greatly improved. New porosity is created through the existing blocks and new infill projects through which the city centre is connected to the river bank in an almost contemporary picturesque way. In this very integral proposal, it is a matter of sowing the seeds before securing more urban connections beyond the scale of the competition site.

Dear Innsbruck, make a good square on the waterfront!

Kristiaan Borret was a member of the international jury for EUROPAN15. He is bouwmeester – maître architecte of Brussels Capital Region and professor for Urban Design at Ghent University.

What are the main goals regarding the site?
The EUROPAN winning projects are an important start for us in the development of an urban design process for this specific area. The different approaches show the diversity of the potential in this location. In any case, the aim is to generate the greatest possible positive added value for the people of Innsbruck and for the diverse users of this quarter. The projects are catalysts for the transformation of the promenade and the building plots from an "innercity backyard" to a lively riverside promenade with new spatially animated connections to the city.

How do you consider the productivity issue?
Productivity at this location means on the one hand using capital of the urban society. This involves creative capital, innovation potential, the production of knowledge and know-how. On the other hand, the productivity of existing potentials, such as the market hall, might be expanded. The programming of the square and the promenade is also part of the production of a special social space. This strengthening of specific site values and public space is intended to enhance the power of urban transformation towards a sustainable urban society.

Have you already defined a process after the EUROPAN competition?
On the basis of the winning projects, key objectives and framework conditions for development with the various stakeholders will be identified. The winning teams are involved in this process. The potentials of the programming, which the projects demonstrate, form an important basis for the creation of a holistic concept. Out of that, an urban planning procedure is then selected, and architectural and landscape competitions will subsequently be held. Due to the importance of the area for the identity of the city, it is essential to us to involve the public in the steps to follow.

Philipp Fromm is the site representative of EUROPAN15 for the city of Innsbruck. He is a project manager at the city's planning department.

INNSBRUCK RUNNER-UP

HAPPY VALLEY

A healthy city is a happy city. It's also a more productive place. Our vision for Innsbruck will turn the challenges it faces as a modern city into a transformative and resilient urban plan that will help Innsbruckers enjoy healthier, happier and more productive lives, now and in the future. Building on the city's proximity to the mountains, its reputation for academic and medical excellence, and the population's passion for healthy living, our vision revolves around a new Discovery District focused on wellness. It will create a cluster of knowledge-producing organisations and knowledge-hungry businesses dedicated to advancing our understanding of wellness through pioneering research, innovations and commercial enterprise. To ensure everyone benefits every day, our holistic urban plan weaves wellness into the city's fabric – from its riverfront and marketplace to a new life-enhancing bridge.

"Mcmullan Studio was founded in 2018 to evolve our fresh and optimistic approach to design, drawing upon senior-level experience on renowned global projects at Heatherwick Studio and Allies and Morrison. Innsbruck is an extraordinary opportunity to see beyond the obvious to create a healthier, happier and more progressive city – inspired by the natural surroundings and its residents' healthy lifestyles. We're thrilled to be given the opportunity to work with Innsbruck and EUROPAN to shape a Productive City of the future."

RUNNER-UP INNSBRUCK

PRIZE
Runner-Up

PROJECT
Happy Valley

AUTHORS
Andrew Mcmullan (UK)
Architect/Urbanist
Henry Lefroy-Brooks (UK)
Architect/Urbanist

MCMULLAN STUDIO
17 Shorts Gardens
London WC2H 9AT
United Kingdom
www.mcmullanstudio.com

"The project gives valuable answers on how the implications for public spaces could unfold." Jury

Left:
Marktplatz and market hall section. The market hall is a catalyst for communal regeneration and a centre for food urbanism with rooftop gardens influenced by Alpine valley agriculture.

The extended roof forms a canopy over the market square which is divided into two corresponding zones: big/sloped and small/covered.

Below:
Discovery Institute. A flexible timber frame structure with a giant roof will cover a village of four discovery hubs and encourage the collision of ideas across various disciplines.

INNSBRUCK   RUNNER-UP

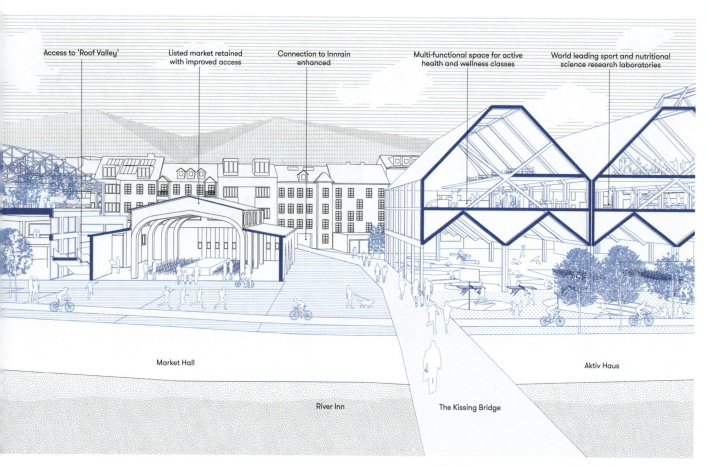

Above:
Section showing the approach to the bridge and its connection with the site and the city.

Right:
Visualisation of the Kissing Bridge, designed as a place to pause and to connect with the water. Both sides of the bridge slide past each other and thereby create two terraced areas, which will provide new viewing platforms for the city.

JURY STATEMENT

The jury appreciates the complexity in terms of programming and its linkage to space. The proposal is explicit on built form and uses architectural elements to strengthen the identification of the place. In suggesting different types of spatial areas (roof valley, covered/open square, pop-up boxes) and working with the 3rd dimension, it offers connections between public architecture and open space in various ways.
The market square is rated as interesting; a subtle intervention, the roof, seems especially helpful for different types of events and is geared again towards programmatic densification. The tilted square is seen critically though, as the elevated view does not seem to add the intended value to the space.

The programming of the productive uses is controversially debated; on the one hand the uses are still strongly linked to the concept of the market, which is considered positive, on the other hand the theme of 'well-being' is questioned. Some members of the jury see high-end uses linked to these functions and recommend an evaluation of the topic of well-being. The project's dealing with the existing canteen and therefore its connection with the university is found enriching.

In general the jury commends the complexity of the project, which fosters the densification of uses and gives valuable answers on how the implications for public spaces could unfold.

INNSBRUCK RUNNER-UP 46

DAS GRÜNE HERZ

The project proposes a new productive neighbourhood using an integral approach in connection with the city. The new vision of the site aims to change the way the riverside is lived and experienced. It is based on four pillars:
1) A network of uses, a map of activities that create a diverse fabric, encouraging a 24/7 sequence of dynamics that bring the neighbourhood to life.
2) A close relationship between the city and the river, bringing the people in controlled closeness to the water.
3) A space for pedestrians, free of cars, where the different activities and uses extend from the buildings out to the public space.
4) A green corridor built using different strategies, bringing agriculture, vegetation and wildlife back to the heart of the city.

„studio.alt is a collective built on experiences gathered from living in different cities around the world, which have helped us synthesise strategies that can transform the way we live today and so design a better future. Innsbruck was the perfect scenario to test ambitious ideas with regards to urban regeneration processes, such as density, mix of uses and circularity."

47 RUNNER-UP **INNSBRUCK**

PRIZE
Runner-Up

PROJECT
Das Grüne Herz

AUTHORS
Jorge Lopez Sacristan (ES)
Architect
Javier Ortiz Temprado (ES)
Architect
Lucia Anderica Recio (ES)
Architect

COLLABORATORS
Simone Carmen (IT)
Architect

STUDIO.ALT
www.studioalt.eu
instagram.com/salt.arch

"The proposal blends into the existing context and shows an integral approach, working with the existing urban fabric." Jury

Left:
The view along the riverside – here towards the northeast – is envisaged as a green corridor with permeable surfaces, returning natural dynamics to the urban environment.

Right:
Visualisation showing the marketplace as a flexible canvas resulting from the re-organisation of its elements. A pergola protects the open space from traffic and functions as a gateway to the area, providing an example of urban acupuncture designed to improve the quality of the space.

INNSBRUCK — RUNNER-UP

JURY STATEMENT

The jury considers the project unanimously as a very serious contribution that offers a detailed plan with a particular spreadsheet. The proposal blends into the existing context and shows an integral approach, working with the existing urban fabric. New façades and the installation of green layers are proposed, reinforcing permeability.

The restructuring of the urban spatial system is done in a subtle way, thereby linking various spaces well with programme. An analysis of current uses, which should act like "seeds" for future functions, anchors the new proposal and densifies the uses. The jury appreciates the focus on the relation of the programming to the space.

The development of additional squares and other public spaces as well as the inclusion of green areas is seen as praiseworthy. The uncluttering of the market square is appreciated, however introducing the linear element of a pergola is considered a "romantic" act to frame the square and is open to question.
In general the project could have been tackled with more rigour. The jury is confident though that with a step further in development this could be achieved.

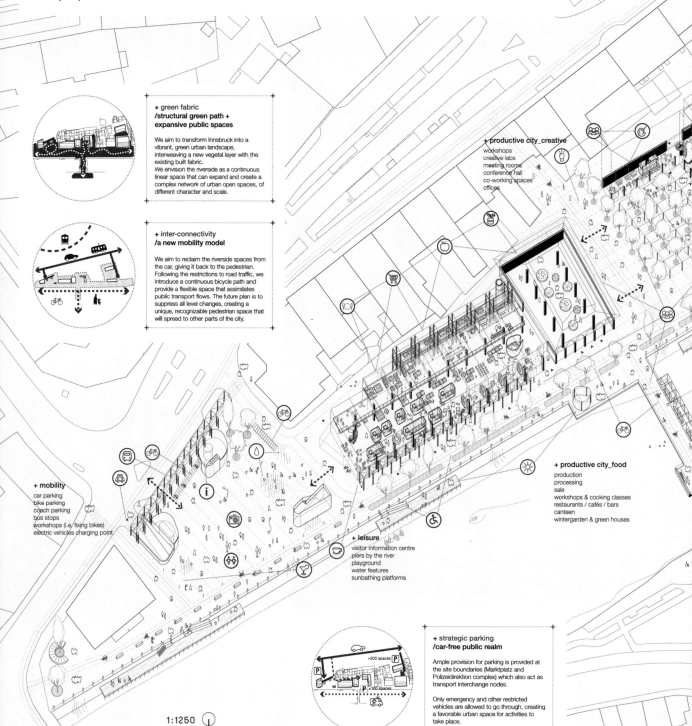

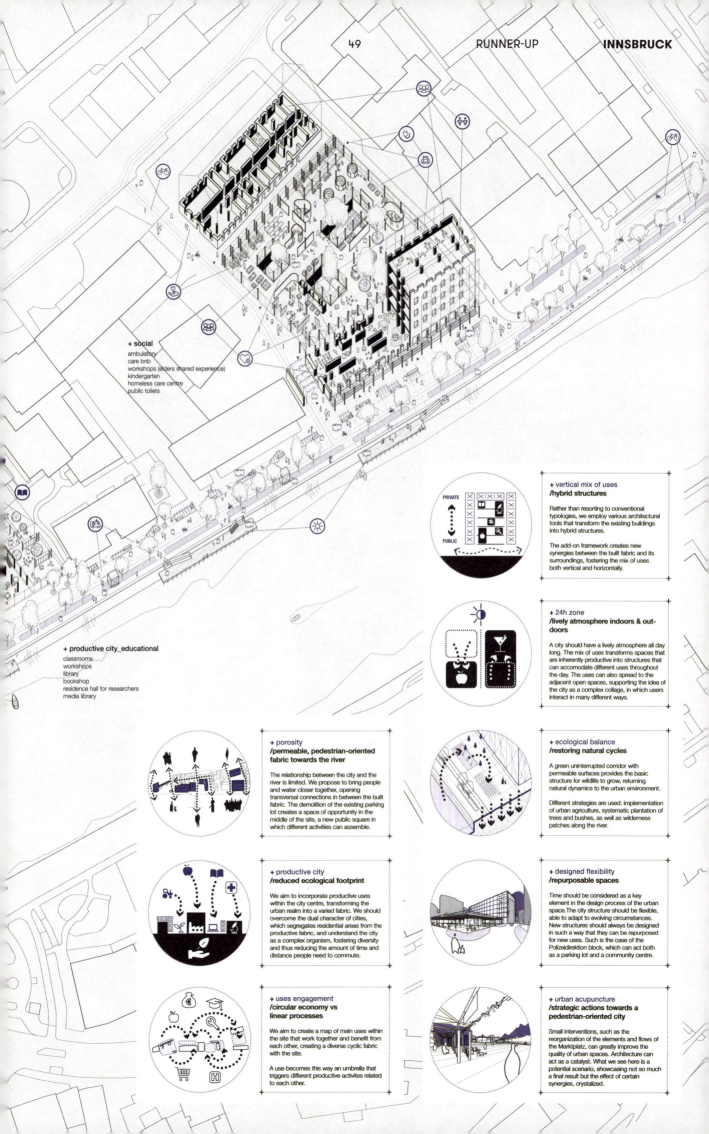

ENTRIES IN/OUT

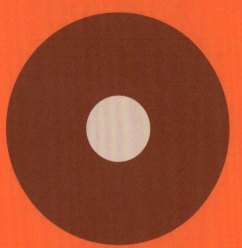

AUSTRIA
IN 28.5%
OUT 71.5%

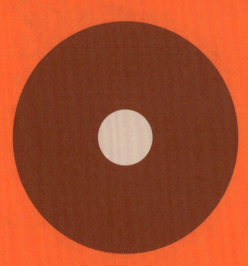

BELGIUM
IN 24.1%
OUT 75.9%

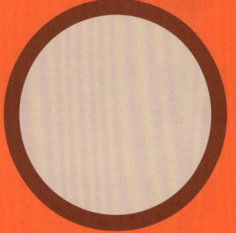

FRANCE
IN 86.1%
OUT 13.9%

GERMANY
IN 73.9%
OUT 26.1%

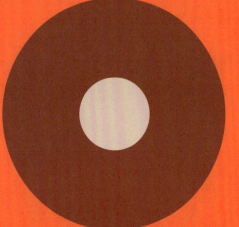

NORWAY
IN 31.4%
OUT 68.6%

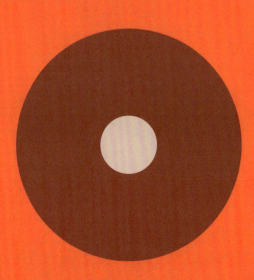

POLAND
IN 25%
OUT 75%

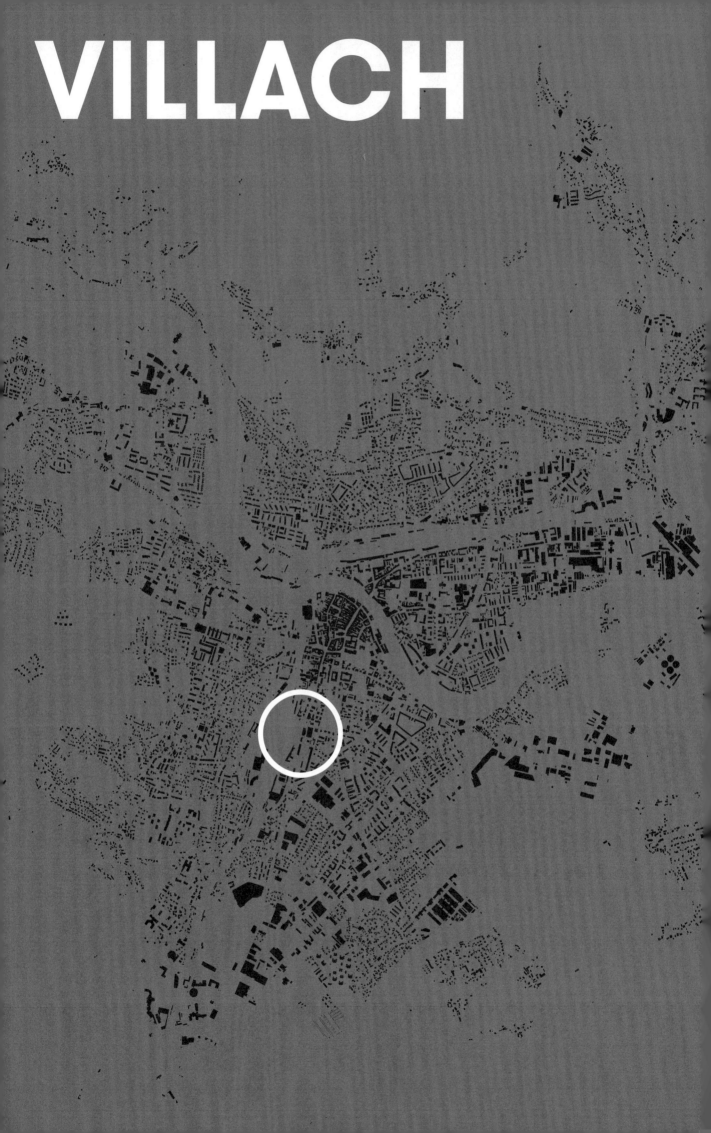
VILLACH

FILL THE GAP

VILLACH

SCALE
L – urban and architectural

LOCATION
West Railway Station, Villach, Carinthia, Austria

POPULATION
61,800 inhabitants

STRATEGIC SITE
10 ha

PROJECT SITE
4.5 ha

ACTORS
City of Villach, ÖBB Austrian Federal Railways

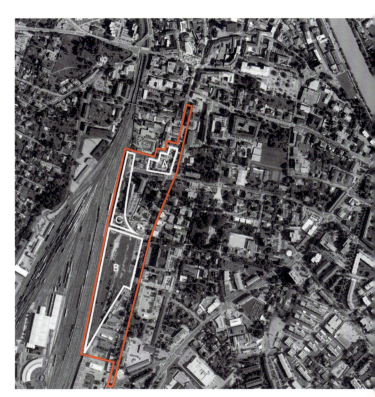

— strategic site
═ project site

Villach's EUROPAN15 site negotiates an exciting position between up-and-coming, diverse suburbia and the lively, historic city centre. Its location is the gap between the heart of the old town with its cafés, little shops and narrow alleys and suburbia with its schools, army base, climbing centre and industrial sites.

The site consists of three parts. Site A is only five minutes' walk away from the very heart of the city – a prime location! However, it finds itself on an "imaginary" threshold between what is perceived as the inner-city's core and the suburban area. Its current function as a car park enforces this image. In addition, the city's building structure changes from a fairly closed development to a pattern of detached houses further on.
Site B is an urban wasteland cut off from city life with no urban quality or identity at present. It is located next to railway tracks and a railway station. Embedded into a neighbourhood with many schools and sport facilities, it has high potential to develop into a connecting hub.
Site C is located between the two sites and serves as a hinge between them. It accommodates the historic station building, which is currently used for social events and will not become available until a much later stage. This means that the project must be fully functional without Site C. On a strategic level though, the interplay of all three sites is crucial.

Seemingly opposing forces, such as the surrounding region, the immediate area of the inner city, suburbia, etc. open up a vast field of potential synergies. Many hidden threads need to be picked up and the project offers a compelling chance to knit them together. With the city's ambition to introduce more vibrancy and relevance, production and its related fields will provide a major driving force to implement a new identity and boost the area. The creation of an autonomous quality within a new hybrid setting is desired. The main challenge is to strategically connect the "valuable" parameters at hand – such as proximities, mobility and flow of people – into a mixed spatial and programmatic setting which anchors the site.

Villach's urban development concept proposes the West Railway Station site (EUROPAN15 site) as one of five target areas for development within the next few years. The ambition of the city and the site-owner is to establish a mixed, innovative urban quarter. By intertwining layers of production, residence and recreation as well as new approaches to mobility the site should reach out to its surroundings and develop into an important connecting area. The site's strength is its immediate proximity to the old town and the existing railway station. Though the station is currently only used moderately, it possesses the powerful ability to branch out into the region, enabling access to and from the city and mediating between different speeds. Approximately 1500 people pass through the site on a daily basis. The cycle path network also runs along its borders from north to south. The city has committed itself to implement a new mobility strategy; its origin should be at the project site. Soft mobility and innovative methods of short and medium distance mobility will therefore be a key driver for this location. Attractive and efficient parking and charging facilities for E-bikes and cargo bikes will be crucial to close the gap and create proximities between the city and its outskirts as well as to the clusters of industry and R&D companies in the south of the city.

Creating proximities and the notion of third space was the subtheme of this site. In this context third spaces can be understood as catalysts in-between seemingly diverse functions, scales or temporalities. On closer inspection the negotiation of proximities and coming to terms with them is ingrained on various scales of Villach. On a territorial level, Villach has always been a city with dominant intersections; in economic, transport and today also in digital terms. Its enabling role as a connector (for example between Italy, Slovenia and Austria) has generated infrastructures that in its presence and dimension seem not to suit the small-scale fabric of the town. On an urban level, such as the EUROPAN15 project site, a similar symptom can be found: a tension between two different urban structures becoming prevalent in the threshold between the historic city centre and the suburban area. Also, in the programmatic mix between production and housing as envisaged in the brief, a new terrain of possible intensities will be generated with the emergence and application of a third space playing a crucial role.

Clearly, the question of proximities has been inherent to Villach for a long time. It is a "grown" fact that embodies a potential for strengths, which needs to be excavated and modelled accordingly. With its infrastructure Villach is now a key node between three countries and at the same time has a high quality of urban life due to its small scale. Possibly the proximity of distinct presences and therefore its necessary interpretation of this tension in third spaces has formed Villach's character and value. It needs to be taken on and translated into the urban- and microscale of this project.

Site B – West Railway area, facing north

CONTESTED CONTEXTUALITY

VILLACH

Blaž Babnik Romaniuk

The potential of a site depends on both external possibilities of development and on inherent properties of the site itself, such as size, connectedness and regulations. The latter is of less importance as properties can only be properly evaluated after the possibilities of development have been explored. It could be argued that the potential of the site is not inherent to it but is an extensive conception of changes that interplay between the site and its context, immediate and distant. Such understanding of the potentiality of a site can be confirmed by considering the three awarded proposals for the EUROPAN15 site in Villach.

One clear and multifaceted aspect of the Villach site is the juxtaposition of spatial and programmatic qualities. The diverse and often contrasting properties of the site and its surroundings allow for an open approach when exploring potentials of the site. Its size and openness (also regulatory) additionally support different outcomes and thus encourage the willingness to swerve away from the expected. The three proposals are very divergent and with this they demonstrate how the site and the brief accommodate diverse understanding of contextuality and the topic of the Productive Cities.

The subtopic of the site – creating proximities: 3rd spaces – was a fitting part of the brief, not only because the site could facilitate varied understandings of what 3rd spaces could be but because there are many possible options where this new third space would occur. The 3rd space envisaged by the three teams could be summarised as follows: in the project *Urban Yards* it is a subtle redefinition of an existing urban pattern to create new spatial conditions; in the second case, the *Thresholds (Myth)* project, the 3rd space is established by mixing typologies from the urban areas which the 3rd space bridges and in the case of the project *The Prosperity Of A Non-Efficient Neighbourhood*, it's a radically redefined space that is created by mixing extremely diverse building models.

The three concepts of development show the strong potential of the site. The project *Urban Yards* sees the site as a starting point for developing a city-wide network encompassing streets, parks and courtyards. Specifically, the enlarged and permeable courtyards, flanked by programmatically diverse buildings, are proposed as the crucial element for establishing continuity with the historic part of Villach while creating new productive/residential urban space.

The project *Thresholds (Myth)* strives to create a city beyond the standardised concept of the urban. The team combined the typologies of the residential perimeter of buildings (Hof) and warehouse type buildings to create a space between the urban and the suburban that no longer functions as an edge but as a threshold between the two. The approach is very straightforward but it does create in-between spaces that could engender new patterns of working and living.

A completely different outcome is evident in the project *The Prosperity Of A Non-Efficient Neighbourhood*, although the team also detects meaningful examples as prototypes to form new urban space. The goal is that this structure of prototypes extends the unknown possibilities of the site allowing its own evolution through appropriation, modification and use. The many possibilities for leftover spaces however call into question the frugalness of such a concept and its implementation.

Implementing either of the runner-up projects is conceivable and could represent a low-risk testing ground for Villach and other small cities where historic city, largescale infrastructure and dispersed city are often in direct contact. Expanding and elucidating the projects would show how 3rd spaces could organise new urban areas and support emerging productive activities or change dwelling patterns. The project *Urban Yards* would offer solutions for continuing long-lasting urban patterns of courtyards by rethinking their scale and structure in order to bring productive and dwelling activities in synergetic proximity. The project *Thresholds (Myth)* on the other hand would show how established typologies could be adopted to create 3rd spaces of new urbanity. Both projects with their sensible and contextual approach present a valuable re-evaluation of the site and its context, the potential of the site and the possibilities of productive uses in urban space.

Blaž Babnik Romaniuk was a member of the international jury for EUROPAN15. He is an architect and art historian and founder of the practice Obrat in Ljubljana.

What are the main goals regarding the site?
The goal is to establish a development which is integrated into the existing structure and interweaves with the public space. The framework for these inner-city areas is already described in the city's urban development concept. A relevant aspect in future planning is the integration of the railway station "Westbahnhof Villach". It is an important transportation hub for pupils and students of surrounding schools. Although the railway station is not part of any structural changes, the urban project should include these types of commuter flows and benefit from it.

How do you consider the issue of productivity?
The issues of a Productive City, with regard to the project in Villach, should orientate towards the inner-city needs. Which usage is missing? Which products can be manufactured near the historic city centre? It will be interesting to see which "forms of production" will develop in the future. The integration of logistic systems for online trade will also be an issue.

Have you already defined a process following the EUROPAN competition?
We want to develop a master plan with the winners. Based on this, the legal foundations for development and the open spaces are to be defined.*

*The first workshop took place in January. Both runner-up teams were asked to rework their proposal according to the findings of this discussion. Upon presentation a decision was made in April allocating site A (Italiener Straße) to the team from studio eva with their project, *Urban Yards* and site B (Westbahnhof area) to the team from Public Office with their project, *Thresholds (Myth)*.

Guido Mosser is the site representative of EUROPAN15 for the city of Villach. As planning director, he was responsible for the new comprehensive development strategy.

Christopher Kreiner is the site representative of EUROPAN15 for the ÖBB Austrian Federal Railways, Real Estate. As a project manager he is in charge of the West Railway area in Villach.

URBAN YARDS

Supporting small production cycles and bringing manufacturing back into the urban context is one necessary step for cities to deal with ecological challenges. With inward growth and re-densification of Villach's old town, resources are used efficiently and a city based within short distances is supported. *Urban Yards* offers a functional mix of production, community labs, services, education, health care and (temporary) living complemented by an intermodal mobility hub serving future standards. By developing adapted versions of the small structures of Villach's yards, *Urban Yards* offers additional hidden gems and new routes within the urban pattern for residents, makers and visitors. The yards provide outdoor areas for recreation, urban manufacturing and for facilitating social exchanges.

"Our project 'Urban Yards' is a future-oriented reinterpretation of the qualities of Villach's inner-city courtyards, respectfully augmenting them and adding new layers of mobility, housing and production. The urban scale, the specific location – contrasting and, at the same time, linking the inner city with the surroundings – as well as the honest curiosity of the site representatives piqued our passion for the EUROPAN site of Villach. It is not only about creating an active new neighbourhood, but also fostering the very heart of the productive Alpe-Adria-Region."

1:2500

PRIZE
Runner-Up

PROJECT
Urban Yards | Stadthöfe

AUTHORS
Nina Cosmea Mayerhofer (AT)
Spatial Planner
Kerstin Pluch (AT)
Architect

Magdalena Maierhofer (AT)
Architect
Madlyn Miessgang (AT)
Architect

STUDIO EVA
Ferdinandstraße 13/2/34
1020 Wien
Austria
www.studio-eva.at
Instagram: st.udioeva

"The proposal is perceived as sensible and feasible with a robust typology." Jury

Proposal for site A (left) showing the concept of urban courtyards and the integration into the compact structure of the central area of Villach and for site B (right), exploration of the same concept on a larger scale.

RUNNER-UP

JURY STATEMENT

The project refers to the historical development of Villach with its permeable urban fabric and interprets it in the context of current and future needs, in the form of courtyards. The courtyards are envisaged as common areas for local residents and craftsmen as well as hidden spatial treasures in the urban fabric.

The proposal is perceived as sensible and feasible with a robust typology – an open block structure with scattered high points. It has high urban potential, is quite adaptable and offers opportunities for additional density.

The park, which functions as a "backbone" to the project alongside the rail tracks, is endorsed to support the fresh air channels of the city of Villach and to operate as a small buffer zone towards the tracks. The jury thinks that the buffer will not sufficiently function as noise protection (especially during wintertime and at the southern part of the site) for the new partially residential quarter as suggested.

The courtyards and their productive activities are perceived as introverted and rather closed-off, with the effect that production is not made visible enough in this project. Its reduction, mainly on the ground floor level, seems a lost opportunity to reimagine the productive topic of the development. The proposal appears to be caught somewhere in between urban and suburban.

Left:
Axonometric view with diagrams on existing networks (top right).

Top:
Visualisation of site A, looking north, towards the corner of Italiener Straße and Pestalozzistraße.

Middle:
Visualisation of site B, looking from Italiener Straße into the new quarter, via Gretaplatz and towards the "Stadtfabrik".

Bottom:
Visualisation of site B, facing south, showing the linear park alongside the tracks.

THRESHOLDS (MYTH)

This project considers the thematic concept of "third space" as a threshold between the urban and suburban, celebrating the qualities of both. While the narrow floor plates and urban block structures of the old town have promoted a vibrant streetscape, the use of this typology is limited to small scale retail, cafés and restaurants. Larger enterprises and productive activities that require large cohesive spaces as well as logistical circulation are consequently pushed into the suburban areas. This project brings together the typology of the urban block with the anonymous "big box" that characterises the suburban periphery. The project aims to combine the two typologies, introducing new programmatic possibilities.

"Public Office engages with the built environment at the intersection of design and political economy. The site in Villach presented us with a rich array of challenges, dealing with questions of urbanity, infrastructure and production. In our proposal we sought to question the dichotomy between the urban and the suburban, reconciling the urban block with the anonymous 'big box' in a collision of unexpected programmes. We consider the 'third space' a threshold between the urban and suburban, recasting and reframing our understanding of the two terms and celebrating the qualities of both."

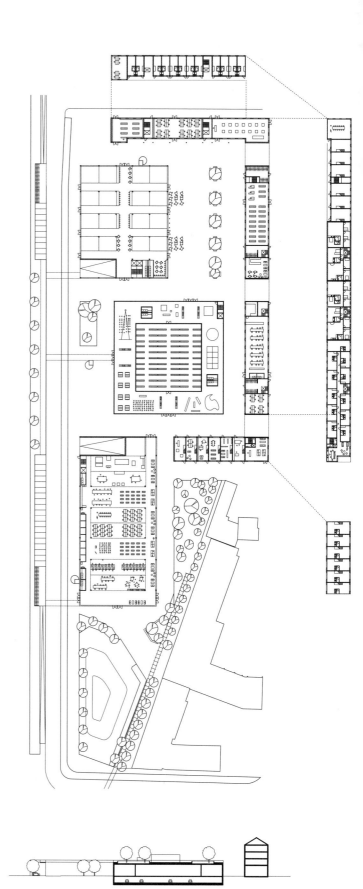

PRIZE
Runner-Up

PROJECT
Thresholds (Myth)

AUTHORS
Leonard Ma (CA)
Architect
Carmen Lee (CA)
Architect
Sean Tyler (UK)
Landscape Architect/
Urbanist

PUBLIC OFFICE
Aleksis Kiven Katu 14A 3
00500 Helsinki
Finland
www.publicoffice.co

Left:
Proposal for site B; ground floor plan of complete plot and generic upper floor plan of housing row. Various proposals shown for uses of box-typology.

Below:
View to the north of a green elevated walkway and noise barrier connecting the new district to Villach Westbahnhof while offering new vantage points across Villach.

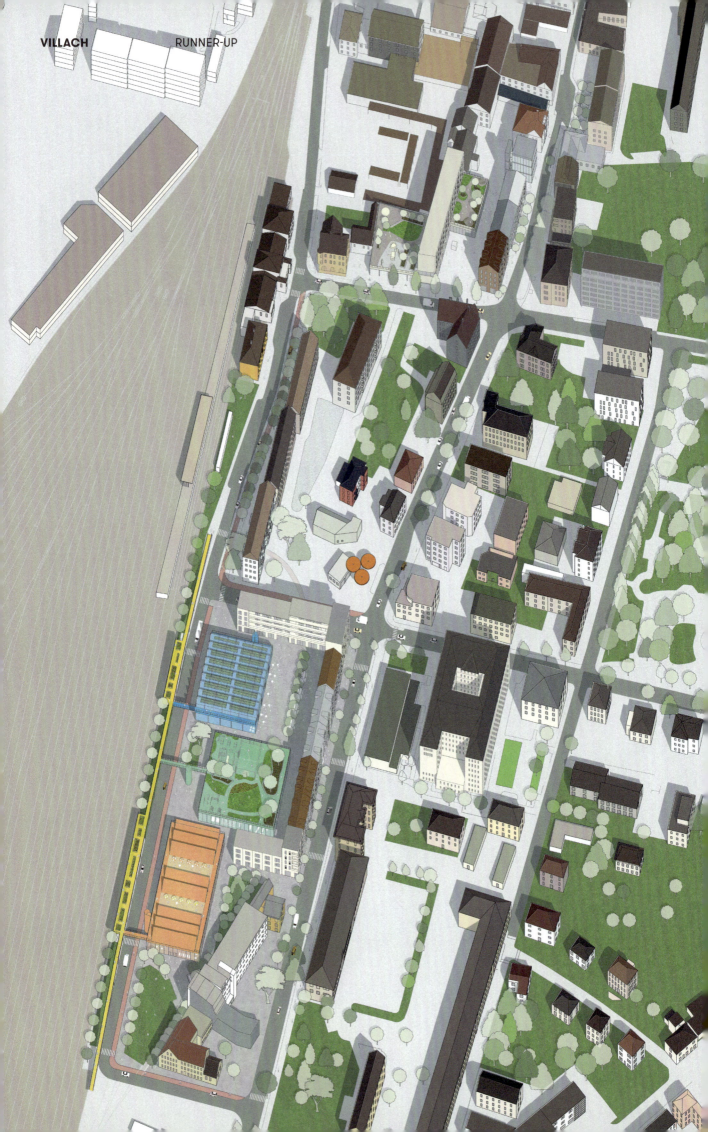

JURY STATEMENT
The project employs the role of productivity in the typology of the town and suburbs as its main theme. The typology of the historic town centre, limited to small businesses, and the peripheral productive activities, which require far more space and logistic circulation, should be brought together. The concept seeks to redefine programmatic possibilities by merging the two typologies: using compact urban blocks, which complete the urban edge, while being punctured with thresholds and opening up on courtyards defined by the "big boxes". The combination of both typologies creates a new landscape in the town, a gap between town centre and suburbs is prevented by the deliberate mix.

But does this combination of different typologies promote urban quality? The jury appreciates the innovative approach to combine urban and suburban typologies into one but misses the explanation of the mutual benefit.

The continuity of the urban edge along Italiener Straße is regarded as very positive, the urban planning approach as conclusive. It is questionable though, as to what the result would be if the big boxes cannot be filled/rented. The proposed raised cycle path and uses for the roofs could be interesting but seems somehow alien for a small town like Villach.

The starting point of this proposal is very interesting but unfortunately includes some deficiencies and open questions that should be addressed.

"The combination of both typologies creates a new landscape in the town." Jury

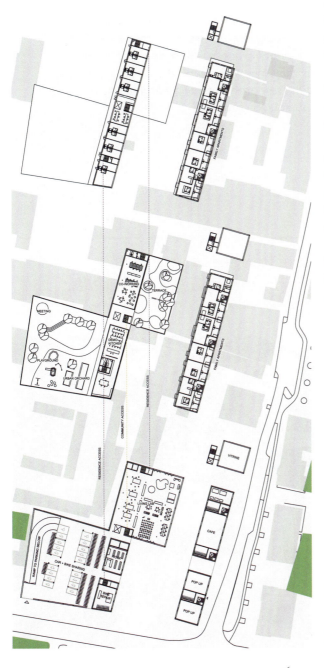

Far left:
Project axonometry of entire site (A, B and C).

Left:
Proposal for site A.

1:1500

THE PROSPERITY OF A NON-EFFICIENT NEIGHBOURHOOD

The tension between pragmatic ideas and artistic interventions provides the potential for our project. We propose a framework that enables various uses and a mix of different generations; flexible floor-plans and a neighbourhood as a system which functions on many different levels and scales. The transformation of the current traffic and parking areas into spaces of urbanity and multi-use will create a vibrant third space.

This project is not aiming for the status quo and is not thought of as a complete and "ultimate" proposal. In the spirit of resilience, we would rather distribute a growing infrastructure that evolves with its inhabitants, the existing environment and changes according to the future demands of a mixed and progressive city.

"The EUROPAN competition, like most other competitions, asks for big transformations – the possibility to realise more daring ideas though is quite narrow and the thinking is too conventional. Therefore, our proposal critically questions the contemporary approach of city/quarter development which we see as a compressed and mainly investor-driven/governed process. With our proposal we try to foster transformational processes and a functional mix within an environment of collective negotiation, rather than finished architectural objects. Be braver!"

"The jury unanimously agrees that this proposal is a significant input to EUROPAN." Jury

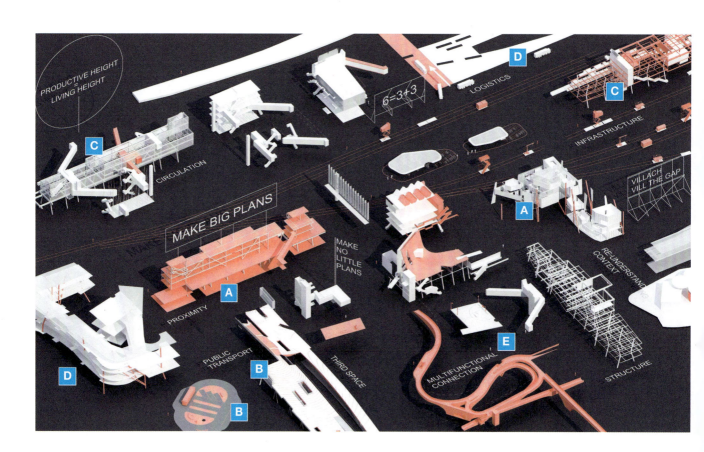

PRIZE
Special Mention

PROJECT
The Prosperity Of A Non-Efficient Neighbourhood

AUTHORS
Silvester Kreil (AT)
Student of Architecture
Christopher Gruber (AT)
Student of Architecture

Simon Hirtz (CH)
Student of Architecture
Maximilian Klammer (AT)
Architect
Jakob Jakubowski (AT)
Student of Architecture

COLLABORATORS
Stepan Nesterenko (AT)
Student of Architecture

COLLIGERE
www.colligere.space

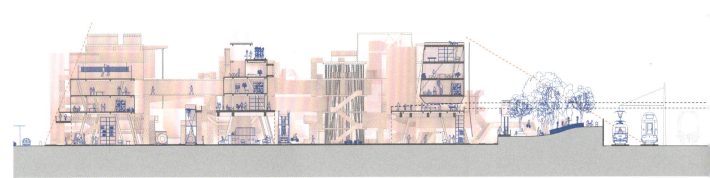

1:750

Cross-section
(east-west), site B

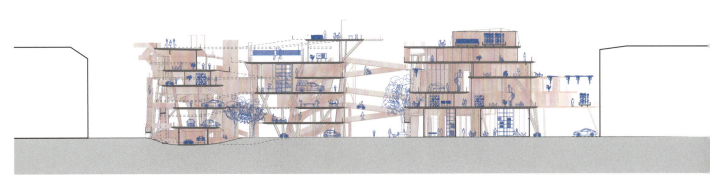

1:750

Left:
Catalogue of productive boolean typologies – showing design elements for Villach, based on current and existing typologies in the city.

Above:
Cross-section (north-south), site A. Building section on the right already filled with new uses, building section on the left with third space uses filtering down from top to bottom.

VILLACH SPECIAL MENTION

JURY STATEMENT

"Big plans" are made here. The interplay of residents and a diverse economy creates synergies and new ways of life and work – a third space is created and calls for new forms of living together. The concept implies an interaction of a rigid structure and its temporally flexible use by actors as needed. Found structures are taken up and developed.

A catalogue of proposed elements and other – yet unknown – possibilities should create a sphere of "ability" for the users. The structural framework should allow for a mix of uses and generations and provide flexible floor plans in a neighbourhood system that works on many different levels and scales.

The jury unanimously agrees that this proposal is a significant input to EUROPAN. The main idea, where urban design should be negotiated and create community, is perceived as interesting and ambitious. The extreme complexity, formal openness, high demand on community involvement and general unconventionality of the proposal mean that the feasibility of the implementation is quite low and the risk of losing the substance of the project in the process of rationalisation is very high. The proposal, as the discussion proceeds, therefore runs the risk of turning into a rather conventional project upon implementation. The innovation is considered primarily to be in its open approach and thus is a valuable contribution to the EUROPAN competition.

Left:
Site A is an inner-city parking lot transformed into a vertical landscape, seeking a continuation of the important Italiener Straße on several levels. Here a visualisation of site A, capturing a transformation phase and representation of a recreational use in the foreground.

Above:
Project axonometry of entire site (A, B and C)

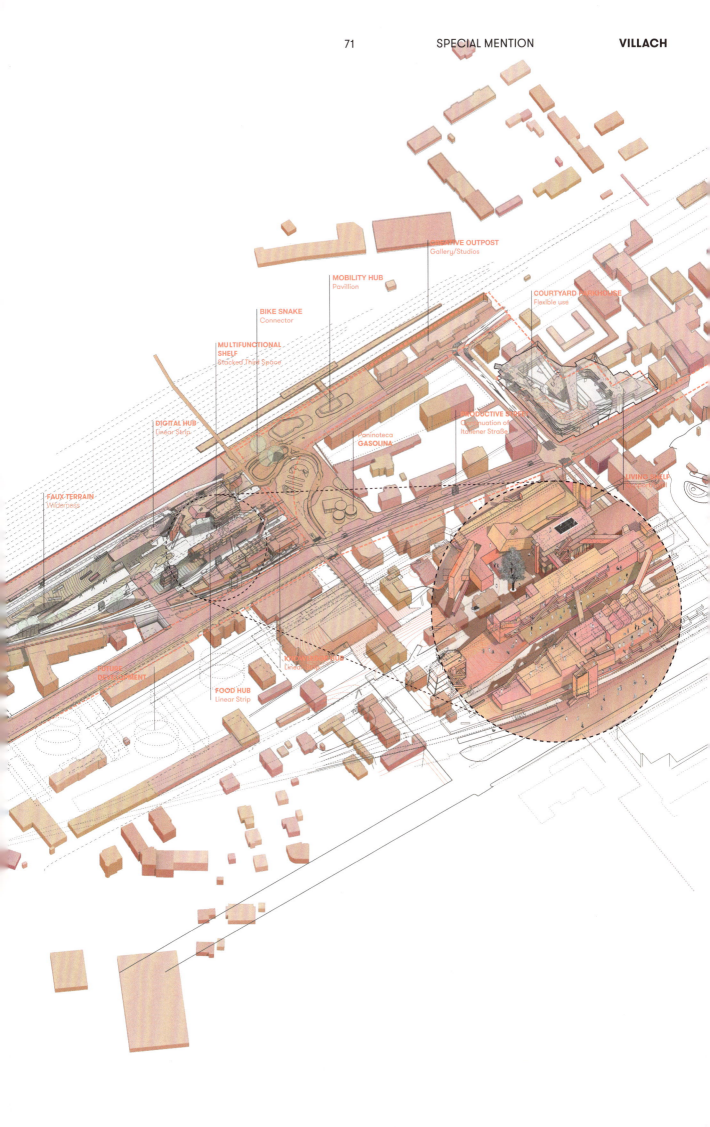

PRO-FESSIONS OF PAR-TICIPANTS

TOTAL PERCENTAGE OF
PARTICIPANTS' PROFESSIONAL
BACKGROUNDS

ENGINEERING 1%
SOCIAL SCIENCES 1%
ART & DESIGN 1%
LANDSCAPE ARCHITECTURE 5%
URBANISM 11%
ARCHITECTURE 81%

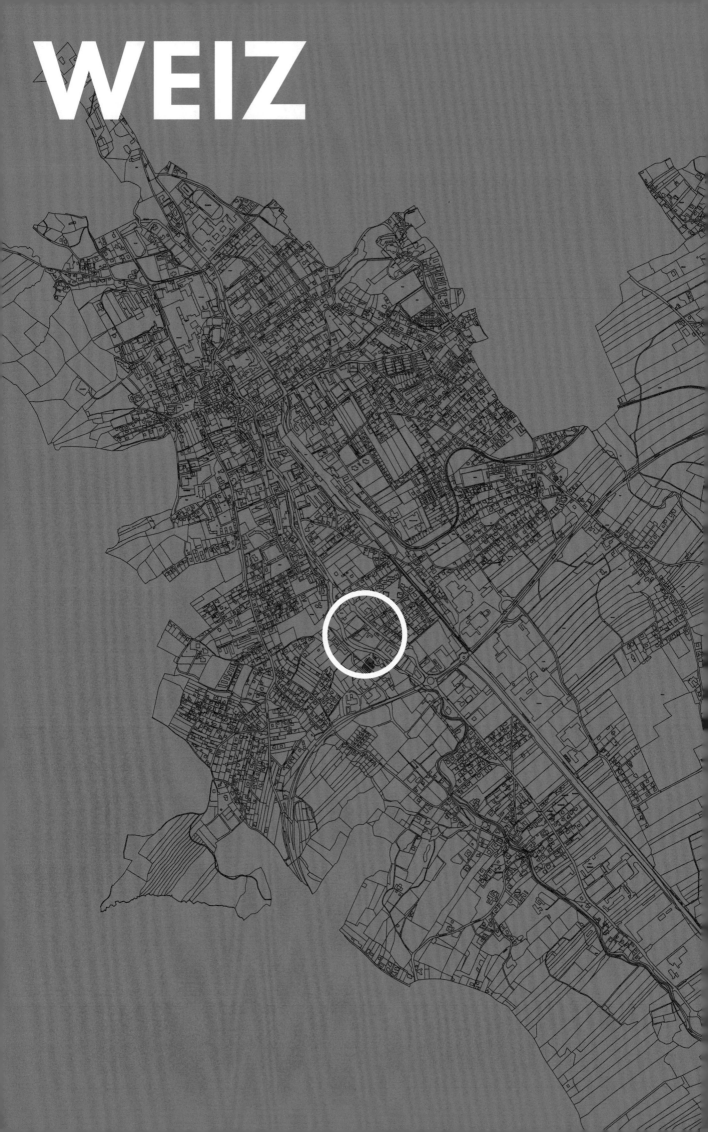

VACANCY! PILOT STRIP ON PRODUCTIVITY

WEIZ

SCALE
XL – urban and architectural

LOCATION
Gleisdorfer Straße, Weiz, Styria, Austria

POPULATION
City: 11,700
Conurbation: 20,000

STRATEGIC SITE
110 ha

PROJECT SITE
4.5 ha

ACTORS
City of Weiz, Federal Province of Styria

— strategic site
═ project site

Iron mills were founded as early as the 18th century and have characterized Weiz's heritage since that time. Business, especially the processing of iron, has always had a strong presence. In total the city, which today counts 11,700 inhabitants, provides 11,300 jobs.

Weiz is a regional city and in contrast to many others, it is booming: the economy is strong, the population is increasing, jobs are being created and buildings and research institutions are expanding. Many exciting new projects have recently been realised or are in the pipeline. However, the biggest project of all is the new mobility artery, which is currently under construction and includes a rail track for commuter trains, a road, a bike path and several footbridges. Profound changes will result from this enterprise. EUROPAN looks at the overall scale of this unique transformation.

Over generations the urban fabric of single longitudinal strips has developed together with a small river and main roads. Longitudinal axes are dominant. The new mobility line continues this trend and runs straight through a long stretch of the municipal area of Weiz. It is parallel to the old country road, which was always the main street of the village. The city now expects a shift from one axis to the other, changing the traditional main route through Weiz. If no action is taken, this old country road with its current heavy traffic will be a sizeable and obsolete area in the middle of the town. EUROPAN 15 looks at this site and asks for innovative ideas and schematic actions. This site offers a unique chance for a pilot strategy to an extent hardly ever found in a grown setting.

The old country road was the main road south to the capital Graz. It always was the most frequented one in town. Similar to access roads in major cities, it shows traces of the typical urban language found in such places. Gas stations and do-it-yourself stores alternate with big sealed parking lots. Due to excellent access and high frequency, the land along the street was attractive for trade and the productive economy. High noise levels were tolerated, caused substantially by traffic anyway, and the location of the city in the countryside had the advantage of enough space being at hand that could be made available for production and storage halls. Having grown historically, the road is aligned with the course of the Weizbach river. This strong landscape element softens the effect of the main road's character providing it even with a scenic atmosphere.

Influenced by this small river and enhanced by the parallel main road as well as by trade and economy, an urban fabric of single longitudinal strips has formed. These lines bring an immediate understanding of the composition of the place. They manifest a clear direction, which seems natural to follow. Not surprisingly each one of the strips has somehow developed its own character. The emphasis on different functions might have triggered attention from certain groups of stakeholders or agencies and their interaction suffuses each individual area with its distinct patina. In fact, the scenic "little" Weiz town has a rich spectrum of neighbourhoods running in parallel. A particular quality of this local specificity becomes apparent when crossing diametrically and experiencing the sequence of various urban milieus.

Not only a distinct urban fabric but also a profound open mindset, derived from historical influences, cooperation across borders and a rich landscape, offer a wide spectrum to act upon. Besides its scenic countryside, Weiz had no other special attraction that would justify settling here. Other sizeable cities formed in locations next to big rivers, major traffic routes or sheltered bays. The pioneer Franz Pichler made the case for the city early on. Despite lacking favourable conditions he insisted on starting a company in Weiz because he was Weiz-born, which turned out to be successful beyond any expectations. Not only did it propel his company to world fame but also lifted the city to another level. For generations the inhabitants have grown up with this story in mind. Knowing that anything is possible – even in a situation which doesn't seem optimal – Weiz has always been sensitive to new issues which could help improve it. The willingness to cast one's net wide, to find agencies, to knit ideas together, to create synergies beyond the obvious, and to break new ground is perfectly in line with the self-identity of Weiz.

The challenge for Productive Cities in a sustainable context is precisely to allow for an open approach and to interlink resources, mobility and equitable conditions. Large sites, like the one in Weiz, especially comprise of a huge variety of human and non-human agents with long- and short-term cycles and far-reaching ecological, economic and territorial implications thus resulting in a complex setting. This site aspires to include new elements and protagonists and discover new layers of functions that have the potential to generate a pioneering vision of sustainability.

The old main road, Gleisdorfer Straße, and the Weizbach in alignment

WEIZ

OF STREAMS, ISLANDS AND ANCHORS
TWO COMPLEMENTARY PROJECTS FOR WEIZ

Katharina Urbanek

Spring 2020: right now, while this book is being edited and published, EUROPAN15 is going through the most exciting limbo phase – anything seems possible and nothing can be taken for granted. A few years ago, contributing winning projects to two EUROPAN sessions at Austrian sites (E9, Vienna and E13, Linz), it was thrilling to experience the transformation from a competition idea to a hands-on building project. In the months following the jury decision, the ideas and concepts of the winning projects are in negotiation, some will be pursued, even chased obsessively, others left behind.

As the city of Weiz brought up a very promising site for the discussion on the Productive Cities, these decisions may be ground-breaking. Weiz offers a lot – it is in the privileged situation of a growing city with a well-developed set of activities and actors, especially in the wider realm of industry and production. Building upon the foundation of a profound industrial heritage, the city never lost track of ongoing development and innovation and is now willing to realize a visionary pilot project that will attract broad attention and add substantially to its profile.

The given site is relevant to the city as a whole as it leads from the outskirts of town right into the centre and thereby links diverse spheres of city life. The longitudinal strip spanned by Gleisdorfer Straße and Weizbach, both of which are historically linked to production, is right at a turning point: it will shortly lose most of its previous dedication and effectively be ready for redefinition – a redefinition that the sleeping beauty Weizbach, after losing its industrial purpose long ago, never obtained.

The combination of the strip with the prominent site of an abandoned industrial building at its south end, which will be available shortly, carries a great potential; the old tannery, that due to its location in the flood exclusion zone, shall either be removed or re-used, is predestined to become the anchor of the vision for a resilient productive future for Weiz. It can be the catalyst for a development that starts right away with the transformation of the river, its banks and the street – and will be accelerated by the redefinition of the tannery.

Two projects were selected by the jury that, although they share certain interests and ideas, in some ways complement each other. Both very much value what is already there, and by a profound inventory of the existing spatial, programmatic and social context develop an overall strategy as well as a set of interventions. Both count on the attractivity of a new green axis along the river and accompany it with precisely chosen focal points: squares of different character, a lookout tower or a fluvial theatre.

The project *Weiz Archipelago* opens up a broad view on the site and its surroundings, detecting various islands and evaluating their potential for future development. The proposals aim for a long-term perspective and include new typologies of housing, whose potential is not to be underestimated in the context of this growing city. Detailed stepping stones for the implementation process put an emphasis on the participation of local actors and especially residents.

The project *Learning From The Future* offers an imaginative vision of the site itself; a seamless landscape from the river to the buildings and a lively public/productive node at the old tannery. It is very much rooted in the context and visionary at the same time – both concerning the spatial interventions and the concise reprogramming of the tannery. The project understands (soft) mobility as a key instrument to activate urban space and by this and other means credibly links city life with production.

It seems obvious to make use of the strengths in each of the projects to enter the implementation process. While the transformation into the new "seamless landscape" can be tackled – and communicated – immediately, the essential re-use of the tannery will need a lot of engagement from the municipality to reach and attract potential actors that share the vision. Accompanied by a long-term participatory planning process of a wider scope, EUROPAN15 could become a true success story for Weiz!

Katharina Urbanek was a member of the international jury for EUROPAN15. She is an architect in Vienna and teaches at the department of Building Theory and Design at the Technical University Vienna.

What are the main goals regarding the site?
Our main goal regarding EUROPAN is to open up new aspects in urban planning. Although we have been planning in the designated area for a long time now, we are still trapped in conventional thought patterns. New ideas and conceptions, which have not been thought of so far, should expand conventional and traditional thought patterns in architecture and urban planning. Young EUROPAN architects, who are not locals, can achieve this goal by using an innovative approach.

How do you consider the issue of productivity?
The planning area is characterised by a large variety of different land uses (as a settlement area, traffic area, economic and trading area, brown fields). The main aim is to keep the variety of the existing uses and at the same time to increase the quality of production, living and trading; creating more green areas, improving the site development of the river Weizbach and trendsetting ideas. EUROPAN can provide important inputs in this process.

Have you already defined a process following the EUROPAN competition?
Since we know the time schedule for the reconstruction of the Gleisdorfer Straße and we are aware of the fact that the current situation and the change in the traffic situation will not necessarily lead to a positive development, we would like to have a clear vision about feasible developments regarding urban planning and design ideas as soon as possible. Moreover, the lot owners of the industrial area will push the development of the brown field. It is of utmost importance to support them with innovative ideas and suggestions regarding a forward-looking development of the brown field that will also be part of a strategy of a further development in urban planning.

Oswin Donnerer is the site representative of EUROPAN 15 for the city of Weiz. As a councillor he has been involved in the urban strategy development of the city for the last four years.

LEARNING FROM THE FUTURE

Learning From The Future proposes a sustainable, experimental and active urban landscape to match and reflect Weiz's inhabitants' creative and entrepreneurial energy.

The masterplan designs both the physical spaces and their strategies with a circular economy in mind, expanding upon local strengths; namely the pioneering attitude towards energy and climate, which has yielded world class industries and knowledge services. The project addresses several scales and ecologies to work within time and the landscape seamlessly.

Learning From The Future is the mise en place of best practices for a life-oriented city, a city to thrive in.

"Weiz's long practice of technological innovation and sustainable mobility really resonated with us, and we were particularly keen on seeing how these strategies could be translated using a holistic approach to planning and urban design. We believe that gearing our cities for flexibility and climate change can be an opportunity to rediscover ways to successfully live together and we would be happy to be part of this conversation with the community of Weiz."

"The project highlights the specificity of the place by linking the single elements into one coherent tissue, thereby creating a strong identity for the street." Jury

PRIZE
Winner

PROJECT
Learning From The Future

AUTHORS
David Vecchi (IT)
Architect
Davide Fuser (IT)
Architect
Silvia Tasini (IT)
Architect

Marta Benedetti (IT)
Architect
Federica Gallucci (IT)
Architect
Maria Letizia Garzoli (IT)
Architect

CONTACT
44 Bramber Road
W14 9PB London, UK
e15.learningfromthefuture@gmail.com

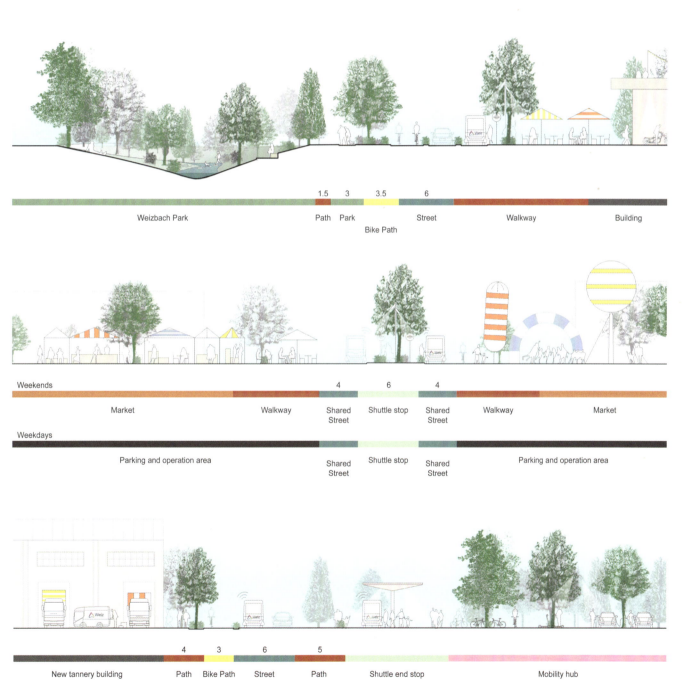

Above:
The backbone of the project is a restructured Gleisdorfer Straße. The section is 10.5 metres wide and is divided into three lanes, where pedestrians and new modes of transport all have their places alongside each other. The street is designed to be perceived as one complete unit although each user can still find their own natural space.

WEIZ WINNER

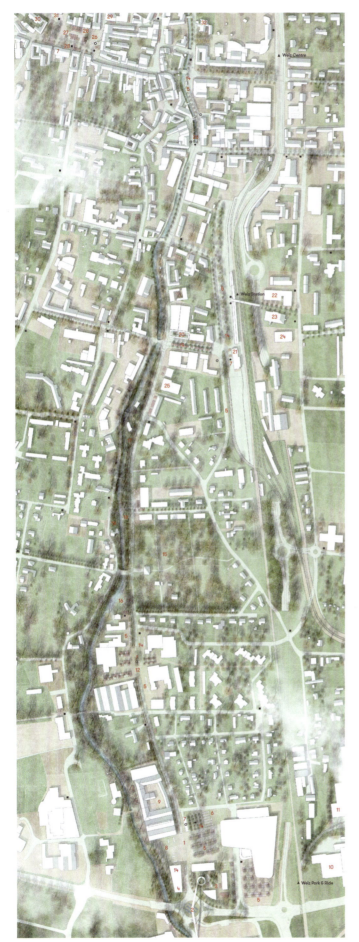

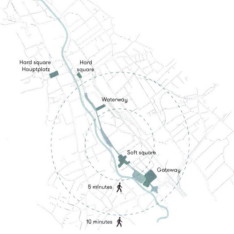

- ■ Tram stop
- ▲ WASTI stop
- o Driverless shuttle stop
- • Shared micromobility point (bicycles, scooters, gyropodes)

1. Gateway
2. Gate bridge
3. Commercial square
4. Parking & leisure building
5. Car park
6. Autonomous car park
7. Infopoint
8. Logistic area
9. New tannery building (clean air centre, sorting facility, plant nursery, rare-earth elements recycling facility)
10. Magna Auteca
11. Magna Presstec
12. Soft square
13. Electric charge point
14. Park
15. Fluvial theatre
16. Sport facilities
17. Leisure point
18. Waterway
19. Portico
20. Train station
21. Bildungszentrum Weiz
22. Joanneum Research
23. Study and Technology Transfer Centre
24. Chamber of Commerce
25. Hard square
26. Market
27. Outdoor cafés
28. Kunsthaus Weiz
29. Taborkirche
30. Weiz Municipality
31. Radmannsdorf Castle

Top:
One of the project's main tasks is to reconnect the streetscape with the river and to find ways to bring people closer to the water. A park articulates the complexity and variety of the green axis while river crossings create a network of new and currently existing green spaces on a wider scope.

Bottom:
The project area is punctuated with four squares to host local activities and support retail accessibility. All of them take up a contextual quality and expand on it. Different materials and design strategies curate distinctive scenarios.

1:7500

JURY STATEMENT

The jury appreciates unanimously the spatial quality of the proposed street scenario. It addresses the road as a public space, thereby understanding the need to integrate mobility as a vital part of its design. The potential of the idea is the detailed approach; the single public surface not only links the green space with the urban texture, it defines different scales and allocates traffic speeds.

The project works with the values of the site and makes use of the existing relationship between the river and the street. It highlights the specificity of the place by linking the single elements into one coherent tissue, thereby creating a strong identity for the street.

After an engaging debate about the need of new mobility as proposed here the jury recognises that car-related industry is ingrained in the history of Weiz and approves its focus. The function mix for the old tannery derives from that same way of thinking – a condition that could promote new technology. In general the coherent programme is lauded not only for its scope but also because it is rooted in the specific industrial activities of the city.

The profound dealing with the core topic of the brief, namely the streetscape, convinces the jury. The project reacts to what can be influenced by the municipality, yet a broader approach may be required to make the street sustainable for the future.

Below:
Visualisation of the new tannery building, combining rare-earth elements recycling, a research facility and a clean air centre. It is a model of best practices from an economic, social and environmental standpoint and will be the hub for integrated and sustainable businesses.

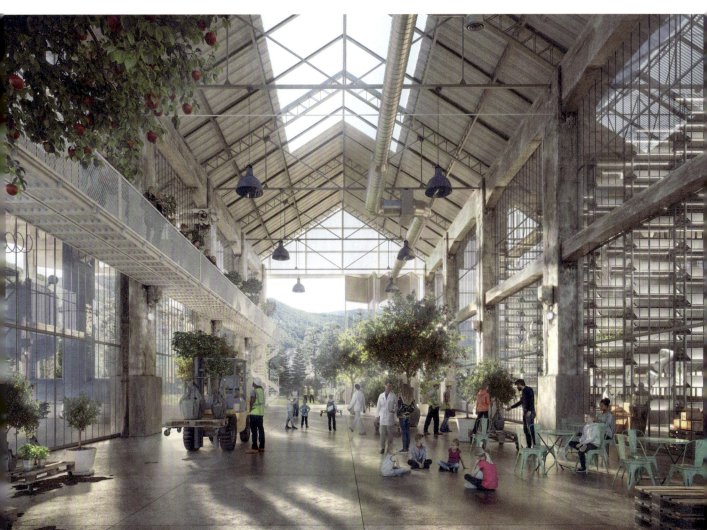

WEIZ ARCHIPELAGO

The city of Weiz is situated in the productive landscape of Weiz-Gleisdorf, a complex system of diverse spaces, demanding a holistic planning approach. With the construction of the new mobility axis (ODF), Gleisdorfer Straße loses its function as the city's main transit route. This change in meaning has to be seen as an opportunity for the contiguous neighbourhoods.
No longer a transit space, a set of emerging topics can be tackled to transform the area. The creation of public space is a starting point for future development. The goal of this process is to create a manifold part of town, whose neighbourhoods are connected by two linear elements: a transformed street and streetscape and a continuous park along Weizbach. Thereby this area plays a special role in the productive landscape.

"We are very happy to have been rewarded as runners-up for Weiz, as we enjoyed working on the site very much. A street as a project site seemed challenging at first but it soon showed that this challenge in particular led us to a wide variety of topics to work on. The back and forth between research and design phases, the finding of 'beauty' in unusual places and a way of reading and finally understanding the urban patterns of the whole region were rich findings which we will use in upcoming projects."

"The alignment with urban sprawl and the strategic approach to it are regarded with great interest." Jury

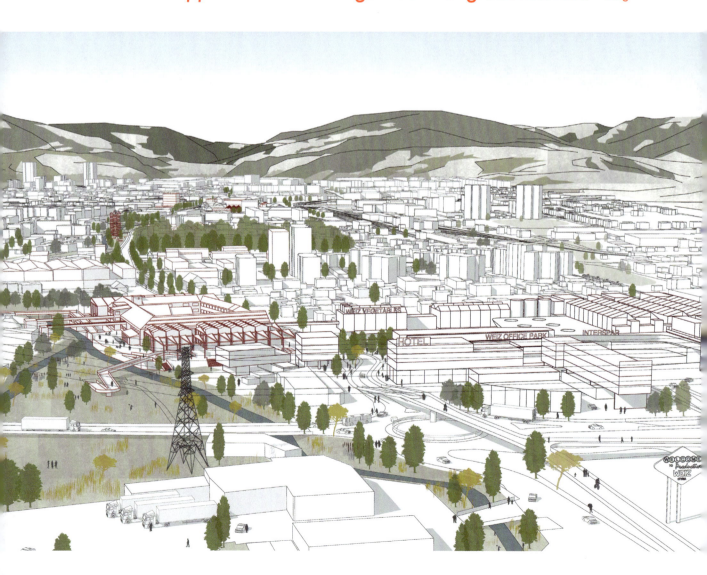

PRIZE
Runner-Up

PROJECT
Weiz Archipelago

AUTHORS
Sebastian Sattlegger (AT)
Architect
Clara Linsmeier (AT)
Student of Architecture
Bernhard Mayer (AT)
Architect

S·M·L
Afrikanergasse 14/11
1020 Vienna, Austria
www.sml.wien

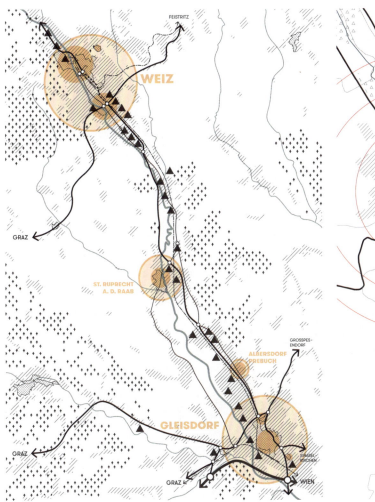

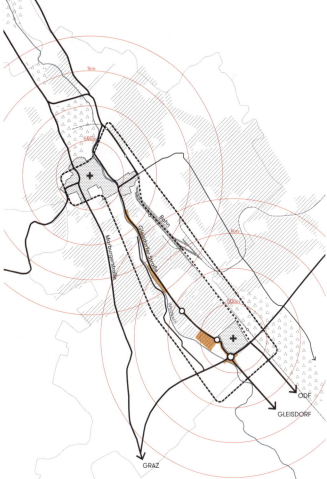

Left:
Visualisation of the southern part of the area, looking north

Above left:
The area between Weiz and Gleisdorf is characterised by linearity, structural contrasts and leaps in scale. Embedded in a fertile landscape of fields and orchards; old town centres, detached houses, farms, huge greenhouses, massive production and storage halls are all lined up along old roads, new highways and the "Weizerbahn"-Railway.

Above:
In contrast to the compact structure of the old town centre a heterogeneous typological texture developed along Gleisdorfer Straße. The Italian term "Città Diffusa" recognises such conditions as an urban form, following its own logics and parameters. The project's aim is to strengthen the specific qualities of this Città and transform it into a dynamic place of coexistence and new urban patterns.

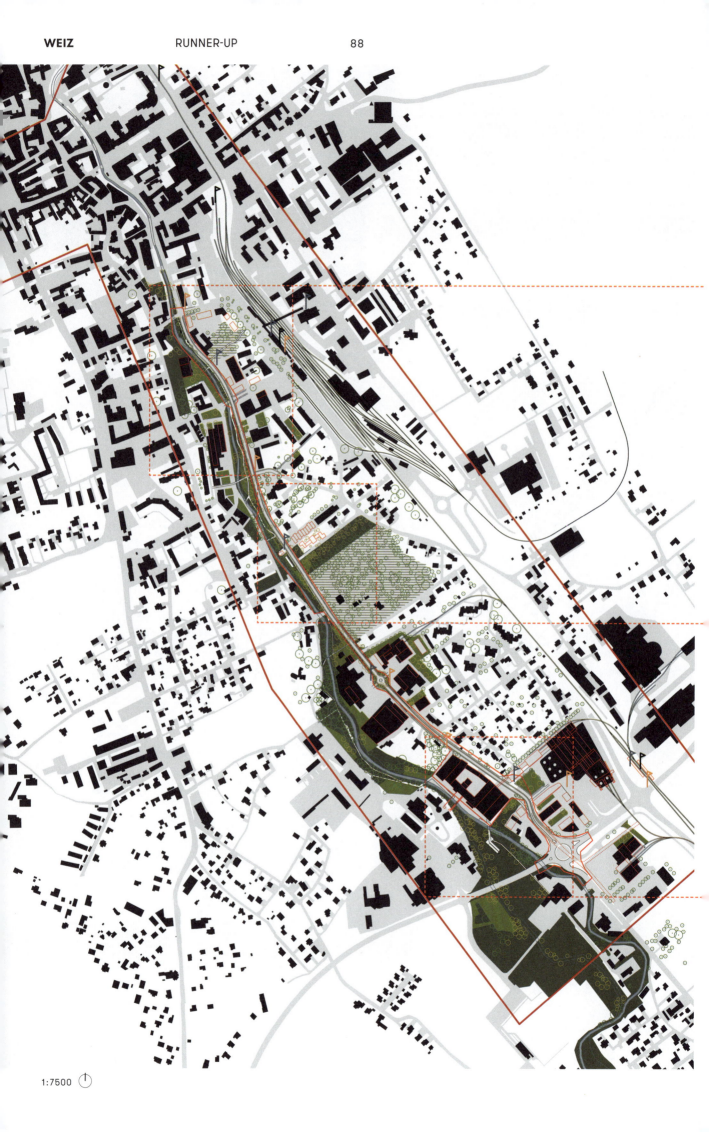

1:5000

The development of the area is programmed over a rough timeframe of 25 years, here divided into three phases (2023, 2030, 2040).

Top right:
Phase 2: Pedestrians gain access to residual space and "Weizbach Terrace", a wooden platform next to the water. The housing block to the north closes and the orchard is now public. To the south a productive cluster develops from extending and transforming present structures.

Centre:
Phase 3: Remodelling of the traffic island is completed first. *Weiz Archipelago*'s Lighthouse, an observation tower with a height of approximately 20 metres surveys the entire project area. Residential buildings and a high-quality recreation area are in place. The forest – still private – should be expanded.

Bottom right:
Phase 1: The old tannery houses an aquaponics farm with solar cells and is a place of production with public and semi-public spaces. It serves as a launchpad for bigger transformations in the area fostering elements of production, such as greenhouses and storage facilities on top of existing buildings, influencing the appearance of the city.

1:2500

JURY STATEMENT

The term "Città Diffusa" refers to urban sprawl as a typology of a heterogeneous texture. The project uses the term to describe the existing urban structure in an "atlas of islands". Based on this, themes are generated which define the development area. The alignment with urban sprawl and the strategic approach to it are regarded with great interest. The project is understood as an urban planning proposal with a broader focus and therefore is dependent on a governance with long-term continuity.

Spatially, the two existing linear elements – road and creek – span a generous, green ribbon between them defining a viable backbone in the area. *Weiz Archipelago*'s strength is its handling of nature and the southern part of the project area. There, the emphasis on the flooding issue becomes especially apparent and is formulated as an integral part of the project.

The expanded treatment of the site is seen twofold: the jury argues that an overall planning approach for the city of Weiz is essential and *Weiz Archipelago* highlights relevant issues. However, it is clearly a project which is less easy to embark upon. By widening up the area, the theme of the street seems neglected and a substantial transformation is not offered.

The jury questions the focus of the proposal, which is identified as a solely urban strategy.

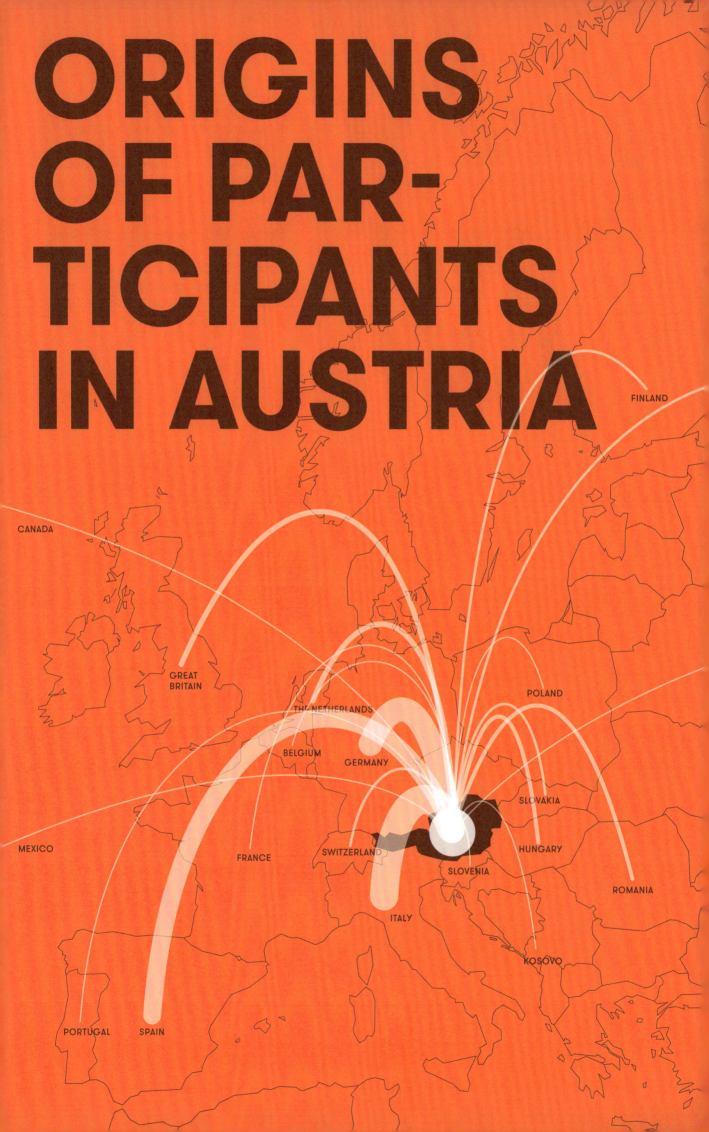

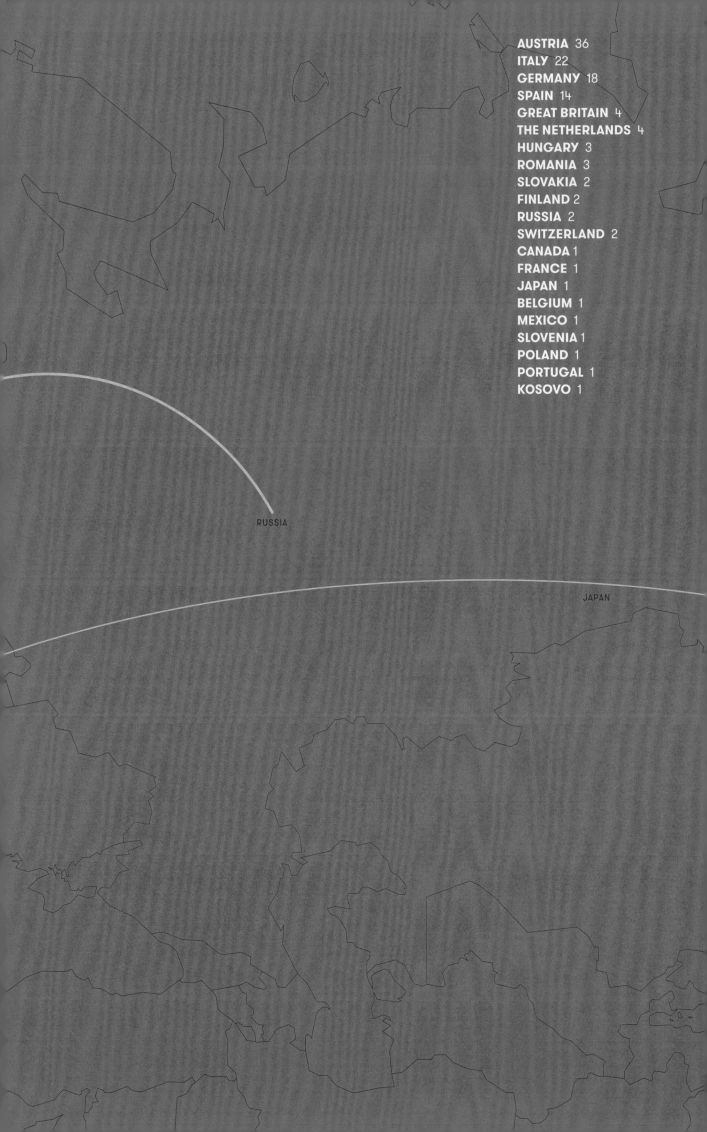

AUSTRIA 36
ITALY 22
GERMANY 18
SPAIN 14
GREAT BRITAIN 4
THE NETHERLANDS 4
HUNGARY 3
ROMANIA 3
SLOVAKIA 2
FINLAND 2
RUSSIA 2
SWITZERLAND 2
CANADA 1
FRANCE 1
JAPAN 1
BELGIUM 1
MEXICO 1
SLOVENIA 1
POLAND 1
PORTUGAL 1
KOSOVO 1

CENTRAL NODE

WIEN

SCALE
L – urban and architectural

LOCATION
Neu Marx, Vienna, Austria

POPULATION
1,867,000 inhabitants

STRATEGIC SITE
6.5 ha

PROJECT SITE
1.3 ha

ACTORS
WSE Wiener Standort-
entwicklung GmbH,
ÖBB Austrian Federal
Railways, City of Vienna

— strategic site
⎓ project site

One third of Vienna's value-added features can be attributed to the manufacturing sector. Facing rapid population growth and a high demand on housing, productive areas have come under huge pressure in the last decade. Reacting to this situation Vienna has developed a plan to preserve, support and promote areas for productive work within the city. The concept for the Productive Cities emphasises the value of the manufacturing sector and secures it as a key pillar of sustainable urban development. Its implementation in Vienna's zoning plan brings different types of categories, one is a 50:50 mix of housing and production. It applies to the EUROPAN15 site and spans the whole surrounding quarter of Neu Marx, making the site a key piece within a larger zone of ambitious transformation.

Neu Marx lies on a central urban and geopolitical axis, between the historic city centre and Vienna's International Airport. A railway station for the rapid transit train S7 is located on the EUROPAN15 site and connects the area to the airport within twenty minutes and to the city centre within ten minutes. Therefore, it has international relevance and the core profile of the area is its commercial use for science and biotechnology as well as media and cultural industries. More than 7000 people work in over 100 businesses here. With the completion of a projected event arena for 20,000 people expected within the next decade, the inflow of visitors crossing the strategic site will rise significantly. Also, adjacent to the site is an ongoing urban development for about 4000 people, huge social housing complexes, a Federal College of Engineering and several car traders. A diverse mix of people and a wide range of lifestyles can be found in this area, where th EUROPAN15 site is centrally situated. The decision to develop the site opens up a unique opportunity to reach out and connect, generating an inclusive network for a new togetherness for all of the people living and working in the area.

The project site is a rather small plot of land. The setting is unique: like an island it is framed by buzzing multilane streets, trams and bus lines with a

WIEN 94

Lifted out of city life –
a unique island setting
with wild greenery.

new train station on one corner. Access is therefore excellent. Surrounded by hustle and bustle, upon entering "the island" an unexpected place can be found, almost captured in time, with an old parking place, wild greenery and a pub-like establishment hidden on one corner. Contributing to this experience is the site's topography, which builds up to a mound of about five metres above the neighbouring street level and lifts one out of city life. Here the site is abundantly covered in vegetation, a sight very rare in areas as central as this.

The EUROPAN15 site is an enclave and has been left unused until the present day. Amidst long-established places, new developments and ongoing transformation the site seems to be untouched. Like a buffer zone squeezed between these areas it almost fostered their separation. This project now is about connectivity, orchestrating different interests and creating a hub that becomes a gateway to the area.

There are physical barriers that need to be addressed. Along the entire EUROPAN15 site the coherent city fabric connecting the neighbourhoods seems to be ruptured. This is due to several factors: the main multilane traffic axis leading from the south to the centre, the train tunnel emerging onto part of the strategic site, a dominant office building without connections on city level, and a difference in topography of about fifteen metres on the edge between the site and Neu Marx in the south. These features are currently obstacles and a comprehensive approach to deal with noise, densities, levels, position of volumes, and front and rear elevations is needed. However, the site's isolated character and its zoning description provide potential that allows for old conventions to be broken and creates an ultimate testbed for mixing.

At present a wide range of production meets a large variety of housing typologies. Access is excellent – key for productive industries. The conditions are clearly set for a new conglomeration where all the different uses find new proximities. The question is now, how to make them interact in a synergetic and proactive way in order to generate an additional value for all who are involved. How can production and living be combined so they are truly interlocked and a new identity can thrive. The project has a threefold task to fulfil. It should function like a seam bringing the area together, shaping and nurturing a resilient community and continuing to do so for future generations. It should be an ultimate experiment for a new typology where production and living go hand in hand while all the different uses find their natural place and profit from each other. And thirdly, it should be a gateway to the area as well as a gateway to a new set of parameters, which announces production as an integral part of a city making a strong case for other projects to follow.

WIEN

CAPABILITIES UNLEASHED

WIEN

Bart Lootsma

This site fits this edition's EUROPAN theme perfectly, as it's also part of Vienna's larger municipal programme "Productive Cities", which means that the relation of housing and productive uses, necessary to produce 100,000 new workplaces in the city in the next 10 years, is 50/50.

At the same time, this site is one of the most challenging of all in the 15th edition of EUROPAN. It radiates temporariness, impatience and uncertainty. Everything seems unfinished or at best fragmentary: a collection of islands. It is a former peripheral area, surrounded by, amongst others, an arterial road and an underground railway station, just before the A 23 or Southeast Tangent Motorway, where 170,000 cars pass by every day.

The T-Center, a dark colossus by the late Günther Domenig, which sits on the other side of the Rennweg, looks like a formation of black rocks, pushed up by geological forces and in danger of imminent collapse, threateningly hovering towards the A 23, its main reference. Its relation to the city is less clearly defined though, as it leaves an area with parking, ramps, elevators and staircases in between to connect to the lower area behind it. There, one finds the former slaughterhouse, now the Marx Hall, the Media Quarter Marx and the Vienna Biocenter. Soon, a new event arena for 20,000 people will be realised on a now empty lot. Before and after events, it will produce significant streams of people moving through the site from and to public transport hubs. On the other sides of the site, we find islands of older, newer and soon to be realised social and public housing. The partially realised Eurogate will house 4000 new inhabitants. There's also a secondary college of engineering and a cemetery. Just next to the strategic site is a high-speed train station which, like the railway tunnel it connects to, cannot be built upon.

The strategic site itself is another enclave, cut off from its surroundings by major roads on all sides, with some parking spaces and scattered one-storey buildings and shacks for used car dealers and rental businesses. It's a narrow wasteland for the most part, with bushes and the ruin of a former bridge, and builds up to a mound that is five metres high towards the corner of the Renn-weg and the Landstraßer Hauptstraße.

However complex the site and the brief may be, the competition resulted in a series of interesting and viable proposals. Runner-up *Der Januskopf*, by the large international collective of possible scenarios from Rotterdam, has a translucent façade hiding a winter garden to form a buffer to the noisy Rennweg. The other side of the building is terraced, offering both apartments in which working and living is combined on the higher floors and productive spaces on the lower floors shared spaces in the open air, reminiscent of the successful "Terrassenhaus" by Brandlhuber+ in Berlin. Two towers contain elevators and privately financed apartments. The ground floor features several plazas and different connections between the future multi-purpose hall and the railway station as well as the Wildganshof behind it, thus exposing the productive activities to passersby.

PLAYstudio from Alicante have brought together all their experience with Vienna, where they already won and realized their EUROPAN 7 project between 2003 and 2016 in the 23rd district on the outskirts of the city, and combining housing and productivity in an even more innovative project that nevertheless carefully integrates the historical ruin on the site. In fact, it's this historical aspect that lends the project its name, *Capability Mound*, which hints at the way the 18th century English landscape architect Lancelot "Capability" Brown integrated historical ruins in his projects as well. He was nicknamed "Capability", because he would explain to his clients that their property had the capability for improvement. The improvement of the site in Vienna, with its characteristic mound, is achieved by PLAYstudio not only by keeping the mound as a green space stretching to the back of the station, but also by planning two slabs parallel to each other as well as to the Rennweg, with a narrow canyon in between. This void contains a series of ramps connecting the different floors, realises functional and visual connections between the different programmes and, at the bottom, accommodates a bicycle path covered by green foliage. It's a type inspired by shopping malls, replacing the spectacle of consumption with a "spectacle of production". Another "landscape" is realised inside of the slabs themselves, as a kind of giant staircase, with public, green spaces on each floor, up to the roof, as a tribute to the Viennese artist and architect Friedensreich Regentag Dunkelbunt Hundertwasser, who equally integrated trees and roof gardens, preferably with sheep grazing on them, in his buildings. The slabs themselves have an open grid plan of 11 metres deep, allowing for different configurations of housing, production and commerce. The brilliance of this project lies not just in its flexibility and optimal use of the site, but also in the integration of landscape in every part of the project and the forcing of an awareness of the presence of production in the city.

Bart Lootsma was a member of the international jury for EUROPAN15. He is a historian, theoretician, critic, curator and currently professor for Architectural Theory at the University of Innsbruck.

What are the main goals regarding the site?
The EUROPAN project area has already been subject to numerous plans in the past, but due to various factors they were never implemented. With the "Productive City Concept", the city of Vienna created a basis for the distribution of uses in the city. The site's good location and its excellent connections for both public transport and individual traffic contributed to the fact that it was defined as a mixed zone, where both productive and residential uses should take place. We decided to take part in the EUROPAN competition entitled "Productive Cities" in order to obtain the basis for a new zoning and development plan blueprint, that is in line with the "Productive City Concept" of Vienna.

How do you consider the issue of productivity?
Due to its location, close to existing research and commercial facilities, this site can be seen as an expansion area for the surrounding commercial uses. Bringing residential units into the mix will showcase the necessary intertwining of inherent functions in cities.

Have you already defined a process following the EUROPAN competition?
The further process is currently being coordinated with the property owners of the site and the urban planning department of the city of Vienna. At the moment we assume that, on the basis of the EUROPAN results, more detailed statements on open questions will be made in a cooperative process with the aim of producing a basis for a new zoning and development plan blueprint.

Martin Haas is the site representative of EUROPAN15 for the site in Vienna. He is a project manager of WSE where he is involved in the regeneration of Neu Marx.

CAPABILITY MOUND

One of Vienna's most attractive morphological characteristics is the presence of its elevated railway infrastructure, whose re-appropriation over time has built a very particular identity. However, can we build another kind of identity based on the absence of this infrastructure? In this sense we understand that the plot itself, "as found", has a certain value and, above all, "capacity." What the project proposes to build is precisely the spectacle of logistics referred to by Nina Rappaport as a necessary condition to "involve the public in the cycles of production, consumption and recycling necessary to create a self-sufficient city." So, we aim to turn this footprint of the past into a "capable" image of the future which mixes housing and industry.

"EUROPAN is always a challenge. In this instance, from the very beginning, we felt a strong attraction to the site with the associated history, nature, topography and traces. We had a vision that it was going to be the perfect place to develop and test an open system instead of a fixed form, an opportunity to design a new diagonal typology which mixes housing and industrial spaces. We don't really know what is going to happen yet, but we're thrilled to be given the opportunity to shape a new and innovative vision into a part of Vienna."

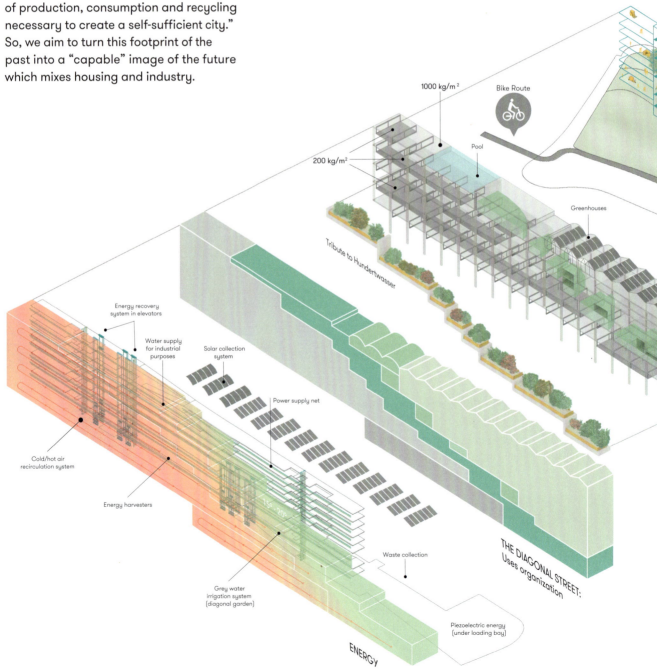

101　　　　WINNER　　　　WIEN

PRIZE
Winner

PROJECT
Capability Mound

AUTHOR
José Manuel López
Ujaque (ES)
Architect

COLLABORATORS
Mercedes Naranjo
Ruiz-Atienza (ES)
Student of Architecture
Paula Pastor Pastor (ES)
Student of Architecture

PLAYSTUDIO
Plaza Calvo Sotelo 38A
03001 Alicante, Spain
www.playstudio.es

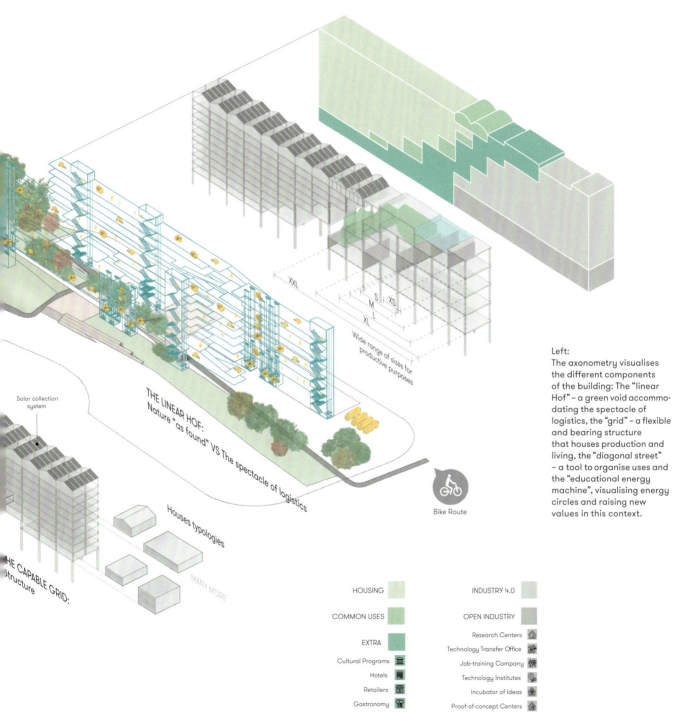

Left:
The axonometry visualises the different components of the building: The "linear Hof" – a green void accommodating the spectacle of logistics, the "grid" – a flexible and bearing structure that houses production and living, the "diagonal street" – a tool to organise uses and the "educational energy machine", visualising energy circles and raising new values in this context.

WIEN WINNER 102

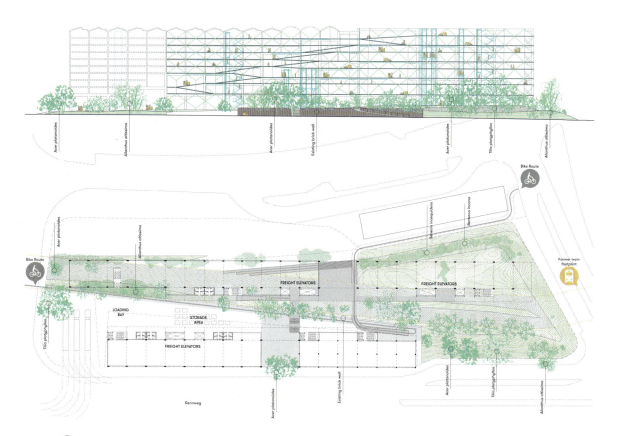

1:1500

Top:
Longitudinal section showing "the spectacle of logistics".

Below:
Ground floor plan of a landscape garden within the existing plot.

Bottom:
The project proposes a diagonal street as a continuous space which crosses the whole building. It organises extra programmes (such as chemists, gyms, restaurants) and communal uses. The diagonal street not only activates urban, productive and domestic life, it also serves as a buffer zone between the factory and housing and is enhanced by lush green terraces.

Right:
All circulation and distribution elements are orientated towards a "linear Hof", a huge void which encourages visual relationships between the different commercial premises.

"Hence, this project is thought to substantially contribute to the issue of productive typologies in the city." Jury

JURY STATEMENT

The jury agrees that the project has a strong and innovative concept, which is well elaborated and advanced. The main theme conveyed here is visibility and exposure of the Productive Cities; both inside the building and towards the external. Two neighbouring discs generate a kind of mutual presence between people who live and work here. The internal street and the slim volumes allow everybody (internal & external) a close encounter with productive functions. Hence, this project is thought to substantially contribute to the issue of productive typologies in the city. The slim industrial spaces proposed create a new spatial framework that can be combined well with housing and is therefore deemed very innovative.

The diagonal street of communal spaces is debatable; a re-arrangement along vertical strands seems easier to implement. The porosity on the ground floor appears limited by the existing wall and the jury recommends reconsidering it. Also, ventilation and light between the two slabs are questioned. Regardless of the fact whether the greenery can thrive sufficiently inside or the porosity is acceptable, the project and its conceptual approach are so robust as to make it a winning entry. In terms of innovation it is unanimously considered the most innovative one.

DER JANUSKOPF

Is it possible to organise a neighbourhood in which living and working are interwoven in a natural way? In which there is room for the creation of a living community that is able to move and to make? *Der Januskopf* is a design proposal for a system that integrates housing, productive spaces and public areas with the ambition of creating the missing puzzle piece of Neu Marx Neighbourhood, linking and framing different scales from urban to interior. Like the two-faced Roman god, *Der Januskopf* expresses itself through two opposite façades, responding to the site's idiosyncracies: a translucent and semi-open winter garden stands out against the busy and dusty Rennweg, while a system of wide and gently-sloped terraces stretches out to the adjacent residential area in the south.

"We decided to work on EUROPAN15 Wien for the complexity and inherent potential of the site. The challenges of a fast-changing urban fragment, particularly the necessity of dealing with current issues and future needs at the same time, led us to propose the double-faced strategy, which we consider to be one of the strongest features of our project. A translucent buffer shields housing and workspaces from the busy and polluted Rennweg, while a system of wide and gently-sloped terraces stretches out towards the adjacent residential area in the south. We have worked on buildings, cities, interiors, exteriors and objects in our professional careers prior to our inception, and we are eager to work together on new challenges."

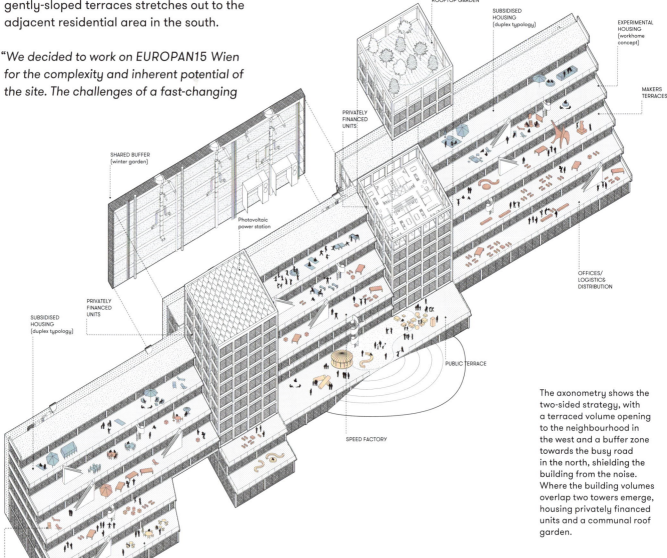

The axonometry shows the two-sided strategy, with a terraced volume opening to the neighbourhood in the west and a buffer zone towards the busy road in the north, shielding the building from the noise. Where the building volumes overlap two towers emerge, housing privately financed units and a communal roof garden.

105 RUNNER-UP WIEN

PRIZE
Runner-Up

PROJECT
Der Januskopf

AUTHORS
Mattia Inselvini (IT)
Architect
Valentina Fantini (IT)
Architect
Marcello Carpin (IT)
Student of Architecture
Claudia Consonni (IT)
Architect

Marco Gambar (IT)
Architect
Margherita Borroni (IT)
Architect
Anna Jo Banke (DK)
Student of Architecture

COLLABORATOR
Joon Hyuk Ma (KR)
Student of Architecture

OPS! – OF POSSIBLE SCENARIOS
Via Angelo Fava 6
20125 Milano, Italy
ofpossiblescenarios.com

M 1:1250

Top:
The ground floor plan demonstrates the permeability on street level with transversal connections and a pedestrian passage opening to a public square facing the railway. Further south another square with a spiral ramp provides access to a public terrace on the first floor.

Below left:
The buffer zone is a translucent and semi-open space. It also integrates building infrastructure.

Below right:
View of a terrace which is used as an expanded maker lab with a vertical tower at the back.

Far left:
The entire development of the strategic site shows the rhythm of the volumes, which is based on current property boundaries. This strategy allows the most flexible future implementation. A green strip, 20 metres wide, will accommodate future buildings.

Left:
Visualisation of translucent façade facing the busy multi-lane Rennweg.

Below:
Cross-section through terraced volume.

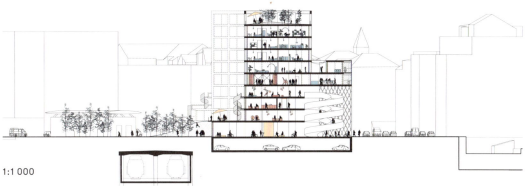

1:1 000

JURY STATEMENT

The proposed project is a single large building with one straight side and one terraced side. In the plinth there are extensive storage areas as well as public spaces, maker labs, shops and other businesses. Threaded throughout are the foyers or entrance halls which lead to offices and living spaces. The production is spread out over different layers.

The jury appreciates the asymmetrical concept of this project, responding to an asymmetrical context of two different roads and urban fabrics. It responds on one side to the busy and loud Rennweg with a closed façade (although this closure on the ground floor is not recommended) and with a more open, stepped structure to the social housing project on the other side. The terraces are deemed viable, while the towers are questionable. In particular the logic of the concept as to how these two typologies interweave is unclear: the towers emerge where two terraced volumes overlap.

The proportion of the housing on the upper floors seems too narrow and little is made of the roof and the top floor, which is almost too shallow for flats. The proportion of the terraces in general could be more differentiated and their productive use articulated.

The jury considers this project an interesting concept and values its response to the urban context highly.

ACTORS OF EUROPAN15 AUSTRIA

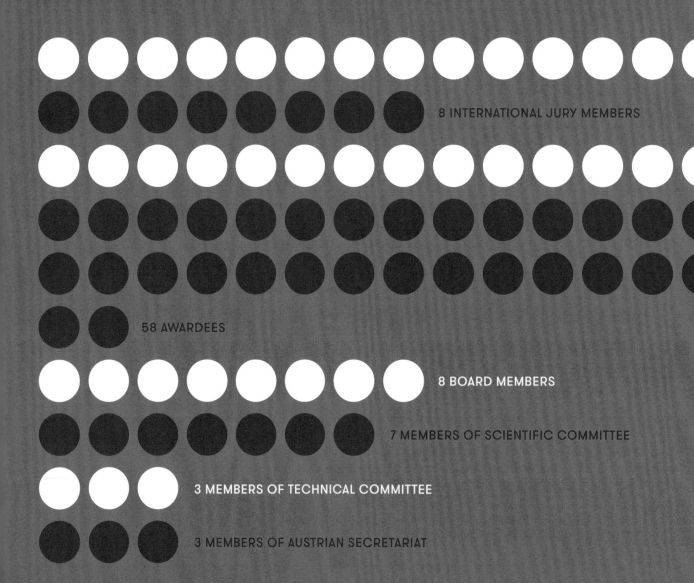

8 INTERNATIONAL JURY MEMBERS

58 AWARDEES

8 BOARD MEMBERS

7 MEMBERS OF SCIENTIFIC COMMITTEE

3 MEMBERS OF TECHNICAL COMMITTEE

3 MEMBERS OF AUSTRIAN SECRETARIAT

132 ACTORS IN TOTAL

20 SITE PARTNERS

25 MEMBERS OF
LOCAL COMMISSIONS

132 ACTORS IN TOTAL

JURY

JURY PROCEDURE

To assess the work, each nation sets up an international panel of experts, which selects the prize winners in a two-stage, Europe-wide synchronised, anonymous jury procedure.

1ST STAGE: LOCAL COMMISSION
In the first stage, a local expert commission selects 15%–20% of the best works. The local commission consists of: three local representatives of the city and landowners, two architects or urban planners from the local context (e.g. design advisory board), two representatives (expert jurors) of the international EUROPAN jury, an international expert panel nominated by EUROPAN Austria.

2ND STAGE: INTERNATIONAL JURY
The international jury of EUROPAN Austria meets to nominate the winners for the Austrian locations from the anonymous pre-selection of the 15%–20% of the best projects.

LOCAL COMMISSIONS

GRAZ
Bernhard Inninger, director of urban planning, city of Graz
Eva-Maria Benedikt, department of urban planning, city of Graz
Andreas Körbisch, K2B Holding GmbH, CEO
Alexandra Würz-Stalder, architect and lecturer at FH Joanneum, Graz
Rainer Wührer, architect, partner at halm.kaschnig.wührer architekten, Graz
Hemma Fasch, international jury member
Bart Lootsma, international jury member

INNSBRUCK
Gerhard Fritz, councillor, city of Innsbruck
Wolfgang Andexlinger, director of urban planning, city of Innsbruck
Franz Danler, IIG Innsbrucker Immobiliengesellschaft, CEO
Anna Popelka, architect, partner at PPAG Architects, Vienna
Marie-Therese Okresek, landscape architect, partner at Bauchplan, Vienna
Hemma Fasch, international jury member
Bart Lootsma, international jury member

VILLACH
Harald Sobe, municipal councillor, city of Villach
Guido Mosser, director of urban planning, city of Villach
Martin Scheiflinger, ÖBB Austrian Federal Railways, Real Estate, Vienna
Stefanie Murero, architect, partner at Murero Bresciano-Architektur, Klagenfurt
Ernst Rainer, architect, Graz
Hemma Fasch, international jury member
Bart Lootsma, international jury member

WEIZ
Erwin Eggenreich, mayor, city of Weiz
Oswin Donnerer, cultural councillor, city of Weiz
Brigitte Luef, head of planning department, Eastern Styria Region
Markus Bogensberger, architect, director of Haus der Architektur, Graz
Isolde Rajek, landscape architect, partner at rajek barosch landschaftsarchitektur, Vienna
Hemma Fasch, international jury member
Bart Lootsma, international jury member

WIEN
Robert Nowak, managing director of WSE Wiener Standortentwicklung GmbH, Vienna
Berndt Stingl-Larome, ÖBB Austrian Federal Railways, Real Estate, Vienna
Markus Olechowski, district planning and land use Central-Southwest, Vienna
Lisa Schmidt-Colinet, architect, partner at Schmidt-Colinet Schmöger Architekten, Vienna
Bernd Vlay, architect, partner at StudioVlayStreeruwitz, Vienna
Hemma Fasch, international jury member
Claudia Nutz, international jury member

INTERNATIONAL JURY

KRISTIAAN BORRET (BE)
Kristiaan Borret is bouwmeester – maître architecte of Brussels Capital Region. The bouwmeester is an independent government official who stimulates and supervises the design quality of urban development projects. From 2006 to 2014 Kristiaan Borret was bouwmeester of Antwerp. Since 2005 he has been Professor for Urban Design at Ghent University. In his professional career, Kristiaan Borret has alternated between theory and practice, design and policy, architecture and urbanism. He participated in interdisciplinary research on contemporary transformations of the city and public space. Kristiaan Borret was awarded the Flemish Culture Award for Architecture 2012–2013.

HEMMA FASCH (AT) CHAIR OF JURY
Hemma Fasch is an architect and co-founder of fasch&fuchs. Established in 1994, it is one of the leading architectural practices in Austria. Hemma Fasch was an assistant professor and visiting professor at the Technical University in Vienna. She was a member of the advisory board for urban planning in Vienna and a member of the managing board of ORTE. Her work has been presented at numerous lectures and exhibitions. Many projects have been highly acclaimed with nominations and awards including: the shortlist for the Mies van der Rohe award 2019 (as well as 2005 and 2006), the State Prize for Architecture and Sustainability, the Bauherrenpreis six times between 2004 and 2018, and OECD/CELE 4th compendium of exemplary educational facilities.

KAMIEL KLAASSE (NL)
Kamiel Klaasse is one of three principals at the Amsterdam-based practice NL Architects. Together with Pieter Bannenberg and Walter van Dijk, he has worked on architectural projects since the early 90s. All three founders were educated at the Technical University in Delft. NL Architects aspires to catalyze urban life. "We understand architecture as the speculative process of investigating, revealing and reconfiguring the wonderful complexities of the world we live in." Often NL Architects' projects focus on ordinary aspects of everyday life, including the unappreciated or negative, that are transformed or twisted in order to enhance the unexpected potential of the things that surround us.

VERENA KONRAD (AT)
Verena Konrad studied History of Art, History and Theology at the University of Innsbruck. She was a lecturer at the University of Innsbruck (Architectural Theory, History of Art) and the University of Art and Design, Linz in the department of Space & Design Strategies. Verena Konrad has worked as a curator and as a freelance art historian. Since 2013 she has chaired the Vorarlberger Architecture Institute. In 2018 Verena Konrad was appointed as commissioner and curator of the Austrian contribution "Thoughts Form Matter" for the 16th Architecture Biennale in Venice. She is a member of the board of trustees of IBA Heidelberg and member of the University Council at the University of Liechtenstein.

BART LOOTSMA (NL) 2ND CHAIR OF JURY
Bart Lootsma is a historian, theoretician, critic and curator in the fields of architecture, design and the visual arts. He is professor for Architectural Theory at the University of Innsbruck. He was a guest professor at, among others, the Academy of Fine Arts Vienna and the University of Applied Arts Vienna, the ETH Zürich and the Berlage Institute in Amsterdam/Rotterdam. He has published numerous articles and books and was editor of international magazines. His book *SuperDutch* was published in 2000 and *Reality Bytes, Selected Essays 1995–2015* in 2016. Bart Lootsma curated ArchiLab 2004 in Orléans and the Montenegrin Pavilion at the Venice Biennale in 2016.

CLAUDIA NUTZ (AT)
Claudia Nutz works and lives as a consultant in Vienna (nutzeffekt), focusing on large scale real estate developments. She was head of Project Development for

From left:
Dorothee Huber (EUROPAN A), Katharina Urbanek, Claudia Nutz, Blaž Babnik Romaniuk,
Verena Konrad, Iris Kaltenegger (EUROPAN A), Hemma Fasch, Kristiaan Borrett, Bart Lootsma, Kamiel Klaasse

the Austrian federal railway company and CEO of Wien 3420, the development company of Aspern Seestadt. She is a member of the advisory board of ÖWG, the Austrian Housing cooperation and holds an MBA in General Management and an MSc in Urban and Regional Planning. Claudia Nutz's professional life is characterised by many crossdisciplinary aspects of urban planning and infrastructural developments but also social processes of neighbourhood management. Her key interest lies in networking the design into the process thereby keeping legal, political and economic feasibility in mind.

SUBSTITUTES

BLAŽ BABNIK ROMANIUK (SL)
Blaž Babnik Romaniuk focuses on architecture and urban planning as well as the history of architecture and urbanism. He studied Art History at the University of Ljubljana, where he graduated in 2007 with a thesis on the history of 20th century residential architecture in Slovenia. In the same year, he graduated from the Faculty of Architecture, specialising in urban planning. He is a founder of the practice Obrat, which concentrates on residential architecture, urban planning and project development in Slovenia and Austria. The practice won EUROPAN13 and was a runner-up in EUROPAN14, both in Vienna. He is currently involved in matters of public space, exhibition design and organising competitions.

KATHARINA URBANEK (AT)
Katharina Urbanek is an architect in Vienna (studio urbanek) and integrates planning, research and university teaching in her practice. She studied Architecture at the Technical University Vienna and at the KTH Royal Institute of Technology, Stockholm. Since 2008 she has worked in her own practice and as a university lecturer, since 2015 she has been an assistant at the department of Building Theory and Design at the Technical University Vienna. Her work focuses on the research and design of urban and domestic space that interprets existing potentials and offers diverse possibilities for everyday use. With her former practice "studio uek", which she co-founded, she won EUROPAN9 in Vienna and EUROPAN13 in Linz.

TIMELINE

KICK-OFF EVENT
ARCHITEKTURZENTRUM WIEN
18.02.2019

SITE VISIT
VILLACH
25.04.2019

SITE VISIT
INNSBRUCK
26.04.2019

TIMELINE

SITE VISIT
WIEN
29.04.2019

SITE VISIT
WEIZ
08.05.2019

SITE VISIT
GRAZ
10.05.2019

TIMELINE

LOCAL COMMISSIONS
04.09–13.09.2019

FORUM OF CITIES & JURIES
MESSE INNSBRUCK
18.10–20.10.2019

TIMELINE

INTERNATIONAL JURY
04.11.2019

AWARD CEREMONY
HAUS DER ARCHITEKTUR GRAZ
30.01.2020

CREDITS

All project images copyright teams, except stated otherwise

12 Stadtvermessung Graz ©, figure ground plan Graz
13 Stadtvermessung Graz ©, orthophoto of site
14 Tobias Brown
16 Stadtvermessung Graz ©, aerial view
21 Mattia Cattaneo, team picture
25 David Schreyer, team picture
29 Francesca Vinci, team picture
34 Map Data © Open Street Map Contributors, SCHWARZPLAN.eu, figure ground plan Innsbruck
35 Datenquelle: Land Tirol – data.gv.at (CC BY 4.0)
37 EUROPAN Austria
38 Google Earth (images: data SIO, NOAA, U.S. Navy, NGA, GEBCO Landsat/Copernicus)
43 Mcmullan Studio, team picture
47 The Schubidu Quartet/Thomas Raggam, team picture
52 City of Villach, figure ground plan Villach
53 City of Villach, orthophoto of site
55 EUROPAN Austria
56 City of Villach, aerial view
61 Lukas Gaechter, team picture
65 The Schubidu Quartet/Thomas Raggam, team picture
69 Christina Ehrmann, team picture
74 @ BEV 2001, DKM-Datenkopie vom 01.01.2019
75 GIS-Steiermark, orthophoto of site
77 EUROPAN Austria
78 Harald Polt, aerial view Gleisdorfer Straße facing south
83 David Vecchi, Davide Fuser, Silvia Tasini, Marta Benedetti, Federica Gallucci, Maria Letizia Garzoli, team picture
87 Bernhard Mayer, team picture
92 Map Data © Open Street Map Contributors, SCHWARZPLAN.eu, figure ground plan Wien
93 Datenquelle: Stadt Wien – data.wien.gv.at, (CC BY 4.0)
94 EUROPAN Austria
96 MA18/Christian Fürthner, aerial photograph
101 playstudio, team picture
105 The Schubidu Quartet/Thomas Raggam, team picture
110 EUROPAN Austria
113 EUROPAN Austria
114 Left column, all, Maren Jeleff
114 Middle column, all, EUROPAN Austria
114 Right column, all, EUROPAN Austria
115 Left column, all, EUROPAN Austria
115 Middle column, all, EUROPAN Austria
115 Right column, all, EUROPAN Austria
116 Left column, all, EUROPAN Austria
116 Middle column, all, EUROPAN Austria
116 Right column, all, EUROPAN Austria
117 Left column, all, EUROPAN Austria
117 Middle column, all, The Schubidu Quartet/ Thomas Raggam
117 Right column, all, The Schubidu Quartet/ Thomas Raggam

Text fragments might be taken from the site briefs. With kind permission of the authors: Tobias Brown and Radostina Radulova-Stahmer for Graz, Elias Walch for Innsbruck, Christine Aldrian-Schneebacher for Villach, Iris Kaltenegger for Weiz, Ernst Gruber for Vienna.

ACKNOWLEDGEMENTS

EUROPAN has acted as an international platform in Europe since 1989. It is one of the world's largest competitions for architects and urban designers under the age of 40 and provides a forum for young professionals to develop and present their ideas for current urban challenges. For the cities and developers EUROPAN is a tool to find innovative architectural and urban solutions for implementation. Every two years the competition is organised simultaneously and accompanied by international forums, exhibitions, and events. Around 50 European cities and over 1000 international teams participate in each session.

EUROPAN is a European federation of national structures with Austria being one of the founding members. At national level EUROPAN Austria manages the jointly composed European programme and acts as a local guarantor for developing new solutions and connecting pilot projects with decision-makers.

Board EUROPAN Austria:
Bernd Vlay, president,
Alexandra Würz-Stalder, vice president,
Aglaée Degros, Iris Kaltenegger,
Bart Lootsma, Claudia Nutz,
Andreas Tropper, Bertram Werle

Secretariat EUROPAN Austria:
Iris Kaltenegger, secretary general,
Dorothee Huber, Daniela Moosbauer

EUROPAN Europe is based in Paris.
www.europan-europe.eu

EUROPAN Austria is a non-profit association, registered in Graz, registration number ZVR-690746338.

Contact:
c/o Haus der Architektur
Palais Thinnfeld
Mariahilferstraße 2, 8020 Graz
Dependance Vienna
Maria-Lassnig-Straße 32/2, 1100 Wien
office@europan.at
www.europan.at

Site representatives:

GRAZ
City of Graz: Bernhard Inninger, director of urban planning
Eva-Maria Benedikt, department of urban planning
K2B Holding GmbH: Andreas Körbisch, CEO
Hannes Kalcher, CEO
Consultant: Elisabeth Oswald, Stadtlabor

INNSBRUCK
City of Innsbruck: Wolfgang Andexlinger, director of urban planning
Philipp Fromm, department of urban planning
IIG Innsbrucker Immobiliengesellschaft:
Franz Danler, CEO
Georg Preyer, head of technical department

VILLACH
City of Villach: Guido Mosser, director of urban planning
Ralf Wanek, department of urban planning
ÖBB Austrian Federal Railways, Real Estate:
Christopher Kreiner, project manager
Martin Scheiflinger, team manager

WEIZ
City of Weiz: Erwin Eggenreich, mayor
Gerd Holzer, head of technical department
Oswin Donnerer, municipal councillor
Province of Styria: Andreas Tropper, head of planning, Federal Province of Styria

WIEN
WSE Wiener Standortentwicklung GmbH:
Martin Haas, project manager
ÖBB Austrian Federal Railways, Real Estate:
Ingeborg Immerl, project manager
Berndt Stingl-Larome, project manager

We would like to thank all teams, partners, actors, and organisations for having been open to travel with EUROPAN and to enter a sphere of productive uncertainty – the only starting point for honest and responsible innovation.

IMPRINT

Editor: **Iris Kaltenegger,** EUROPAN Austria
Copy editing, proofreading: **Catriona Low**
Design and lithography: **sensomatic**
Printing and binding: **Medienfabrik Graz**

© 2020 EUROPAN Austria, Graz, and Park Books AG, Zurich

© For the texts: the authors
© For the images: the architects and photographers

Park Books
Niederdorfstrasse 54
8001 Zurich
Switzerland
www.park-books.com

Park Books is being supported by the Federal Office of Culture with a general subsidy for the years 2016–2020.

All rights reserved; no part of this publication may be reproduced, stored in a retrieval system or transmitted in any form or by any means, electronic, mechanical, photocopying, recording, or otherwise, without the prior written consent of the publisher.

ISBN 978-3-03860-212-5

EUROPAN Austria is being supported by the Ministry of the Federal Republic of Austria for Arts, Culture, Civil Service and Sport.

Bundesministerium
Kunst, Kultur,
öffentlicher Dienst und Sport